D0760245

Rockhounding Nevada

Help Us Keep This Guide Up to Date

Every effort has been made by the author and editors to make this guide as accurate and useful as possible. However, many things can change after a guide is published—roads are detoured, phone numbers change, facilities come under new management, etc.

We would love to hear from you concerning your experiences with this guide and how you feel it could be improved and kept up to date. While we may not be able to respond to all comments and suggestions, we'll take them to heart and we'll also make certain to share them with the author. Please send your comments and suggestions to the following address:

Globe Pequot Press
Reader Response/Editorial Department
P.O. Box 480
Guilford, CT 06437

Or you may e-mail us at:

editorial@GlobePequot.com

Thanks for your input, and happy rockhounding!

Rockhounding Nevada

A Guide to the State's Best Rockhounding Sites

Second Edition

William A. Kappele

FALCONGUIDES

GUILFORD, CONNECTICUT
HELENA, MONTANA
AN IMPRINT OF GLOBE PEQUOT PRESS

To buy books in quantity for corporate use
or incentives, call **(800) 962–0973**
or e-mail **premiums@GlobePequot.com.**

FALCONGUIDES®

Copyright © 1998, 2011 by Morris Book Publishing, LLC

ALL RIGHTS RESERVED. No part of this book may be reproduced or transmitted in any form by any means, electronic or mechanical, including photocopying and recording, or by any information storage and retrieval system, except as may be expressly permitted in writing from the publisher. Requests for permission should be addressed to Globe Pequot Press, Attn: Rights and Permissions Department, P.O. Box 480, Guilford, Connecticut 06437.

FalconGuides is an imprint of Globe Pequot Press.
Falcon, FalconGuides, and Outfit Your Mind are registered trademarks of Morris Book Publishing, LLC.

Photography by William A. Kappele
Layout: Sue Murray
Project editor: Gregory Hyman
Maps © Morris Book Publishing, LLC

TOPO! Explorer software and SuperQuad source maps courtesy of National Geographic Maps. For information about TOPO! Explorer, TOPO!, and Nat Geo Maps products, to to www.topo.com or www.natgeomaps.com.

Library of Congress Cataloging-in-Publication Data

Kappele, William A., 1931-
  Rockhounding Nevada : a guide to the state's best rockhounding sites / William A. Kappele. — 2nd ed.
     p. cm.
  ISBN 978-0-7627-7142-4
  1. Rocks—Collection and preservation—Nevada—Guidebooks. 2. Nevada—Guidebooks.
I. Title.
  QE445.N3K36 2011
  552.09793—dc23

                                                        2011026489

Printed in the United States of America
10 9 8 7 6 5 4 3

The author and Globe Pequot Press assume no liability for accidents happening to, or injuries sustained by, readers who engage in the activities described in this book.

In memory of Cora Gustavson Kappele
My world has grown cold without your smile to warm it

N

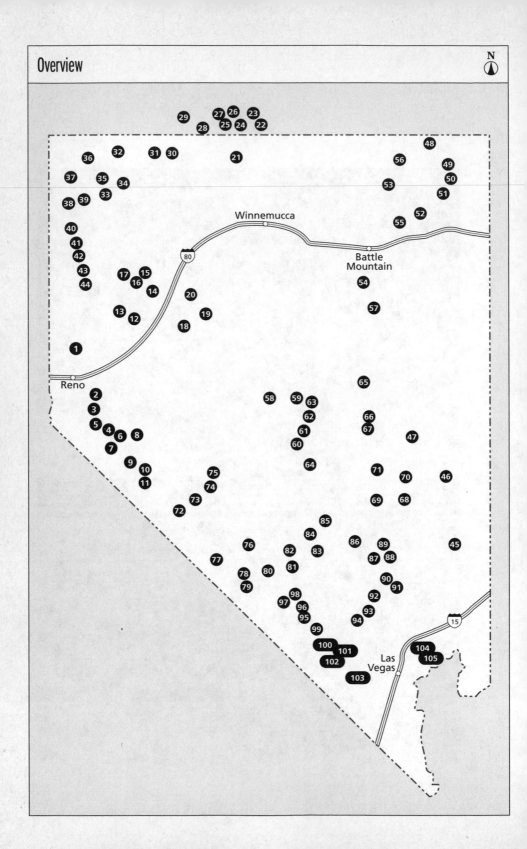

Contents

The Sites

Acknowledgments

It takes the input of a lot of people to write a book like this, and I am always afraid of leaving someone out when acknowledging their help. If I forgot anyone here, feel free to go find a rock and throw it at me.

I have included acknowledgments from the first edition, since without all of the folks mentioned then, not only would there have been no first edition but, obviously, there would have been no second edition either.

First, let me thank the many, many folks in motels, gas stations, restaurants, information booths, gift shops, bookstores, rock shops, and all of the other places where my wife, Cora, and I met people who, in the course of conversation, gave us hints and tips on where to look for rocks. Without this kind of help, I would still be wandering around in the wilds of Nevada stooping and tossing.

I am once again indebted to the fine folks at all of the Bureau of Land Management (BLM) and USDA Forest Service offices for their help and good humor in answering my questions. It seems to have become fashionable in some circles to paint these folks as uncaring bureaucrats whose sole mission in life is to make our lives miserable. My experience has been quite the opposite. Cora and I dealt with these good people for years, and I cannot remember anyone who was less than completely friendly and helpful.

Thanks to the young man in the Pizza Hut in Carson City who told me about a site in the mountains west of town.

One of the best places to start looking for rocks in a new place is at the local chamber of commerce. My thanks to chamber folks in Lyon County, Sparks, Pahrump Valley, Tonopah, Pershing County, and Fernley. They sent me maps, brochures, and even some names of local rockhounds to contact.

Thanks, of course, to W. R. C. Shedenhelm, editor emeritus of *Rock & Gem* magazine. He was the first one to publish one of my rockhound articles, which encouraged me to continue to ramble on in print. He still keeps me honest by correcting my very rare misspellings.

Once again, megathanks to Gary Curtiss, a geologist with the Colorado Department of Natural Resources, for his invaluable help in identifying mineral specimens. This would have been a shorter book without his expertise.

Finally, I give deepest thanks to Cora, who visited every site in the first edition (and a whole lot more) with me, and kept me focused on the task at hand. Without her help I would have forgotten to write down many of the mileages and altitudes. She also reminded me, after long days of driving down bumpy,

It's nice to rockhound in a state that puts up signs.

dirt roads that yielded only dust and gnats, that there would be a tomorrow, and that one may, indeed, find the Hope agate.

For this edition, I once again have to thank all of the friendly and helpful folks at the BLM. They filled me in on the cleanup at the Texas Spring site and pointed me to several of the new sites. My next thank you is to the Internet, which provided me with all kinds of ideas for rockhounding sites. Some paid off and others didn't, but on balance it was a big plus.

Without doubt, though, the most important person who helped get this book researched was my son Richard. He accompanied me to well over one hundred sites over a course of nearly 6,000 miles and kept me on track, took GPS readings, drew the rough maps, recorded mileages, and in short did all of the stuff that I generally mess up. Without him, I could not have done this book. Thank you, Richard.

About This Book

Anyone who has followed the rockhound hobby for more than a few years has surely encountered the two most common types of guidebooks. First is the one that simply gives a rough map with approximate locations of various rocks and minerals. This is wonderful if you have the time and the inclination to drive up and down thousands of miles of dirt roads searching for the right site. Most of us, however, like to get within striking distance without spending a whole vacation looking for it.

The second type of guidebook looks more like a reference work for descriptive adjectives. Although the material at a given site may look like a piece of broken sidewalk, it will often be described as "fiery red," "deep, rich purple," or "breathtaking orange." Many rockhounds (including yours truly) have driven down miles of dusty roads and hiked up lots of steep hills only to be disappointed because the author's enthusiasm outdid the actual beauty of the find. I will try not to mislead you in this manner. If a material is red, I will call it that even if I think it is "fiery." If I think some sample or other is especially nice, I may say so, but you will have to be the ultimate judge, since beauty certainly is in the eye of the beholder.

Another problem with some guidebooks is that they have been reprinted many times, but the sites have not been rechecked. Thus, a rockhound could find that the listed site is now home to a shopping center or that the material left after years of hunting would not be enough for one small earring. This is not to say that all old sites are worked out or covered up, however. Many are still productive after more than fifty years of rockhounding, but it often takes more than just leaning out the car window and picking up samples. I have many of the good, old sites in this book, but I will tell you just how much you can expect to find and how hard you will have to work for your prize specimens.

For the first edition, Cora and I visited each of the sites in the book (with the exception of the Trips for the Intrepid Explorer section) during the fall and winter of 1996. The purpose was to ensure that you would not be disappointed, and that what we said was at a site actually was. Of course, I knew that if you should be reading the 1996 edition in the year 3000, I couldn't guarantee that you wouldn't find shopping malls and empty holes in the ground where we said the rocks were. I was also as careful as humanly possible not to send you onto private land or working mines.

These were also my goals for this second edition. Consequently, I revisited all of the original sites, removed a few that were closed to collecting, or were, in my opinion, no longer productive enough to send you out there. I added quite a few new sites, and most important of all, I supplied the GPS coordinates for each site to make finding it significantly easier in a state with an often confusing array of intersecting dirt roads, tracks, and trails.

Nevada is so vast and remote that much of the time it is not possible to tell for certain just who a property belongs to. Most of the state is comprised of federal lands, with much of it administered by the Bureau of Land Management (BLM). But there are tracts throughout BLM lands that are private. The best rule of thumb is that if the land is not posted otherwise, it is okay to rockhound. If land is fenced, but not posted, and the gates are not locked, it is okay to rockhound. Remember to leave gates as you find them. If a gate was closed, close it. If it was open, leave it open.

Mines are bigger problems, since they change ownership often and may be abandoned one day and working the next due to fluctuations in mineral prices and the whims (and cash flow) of their owners. Consequently, if a trip to a mine is a long or rough one, it is a good idea to inquire locally before starting out. You may save a lot of time, effort, and frustration.

I also feel there is a lot more to rockhounding than just filling up the car trunk with rocks and hauling them home to the backyard. The facets (no pun intended) of the hobby are many and varied. There are collectors who just want pretty rocks to display in a rock garden. Often, these folks don't know what the material really is. That's fine. Some other rockhounds are locked into agates and jaspers and would walk over a mountain of mineral specimens, not even seeing them, in order to get to their particular favorites. Some collect only what they can use their lapidary skills on and others want only mineral specimens for display or micromounting. There are also those whose interest is in geology and who don't really care if the rock looks like used brick or the Hope diamond. In short, rockhounds come in all flavors, and we have tried to include something for all of them.

Speaking of flavors, some of you dyed-in-the-wool turquoisians may wonder why I have not included any turquoise sites. As many of you may know, Nevada has been a major producer of turquoise for a long time. The problem is that much like gold mines, turquoise mines are off-limits to rockhounds when they are producing. And when they are abandoned, it is because there is no more turquoise. Does that come as a surprise? Of course, you can probably find a few chips on the tailings to carry home in a pill bottle, but the chances are that the pills were more valuable.

Finally, I want to make it clear that this book only scratches the surface of the sites available in Nevada. I hope I can get you to sites that will be productive in areas where much more can be found. If you have time, explore the surrounding countryside and talk to local folks in motels, restaurants, gas stations, rock shops, gift shops, and any place else in the area. Good tips are often found in the most unlikely places. To find good stones, leave no stone unturned.

Introduction: Welcome to Nevada

It seems that everyone who writes about any area describes it as "paradise." Such-and-such river is a fisherman's paradise. So-and-so mountain is a rock climber's paradise. This-and-that mall is a shopper's paradise. I am afraid that I will have to fall into the trap and describe Nevada as a rockhound's paradise.

I don't know just what the definition of such a paradise should be, but if you consider an area where you can find something of interest to the rockhound just about anywhere you go a paradise, then Nevada qualifies. If you think that being able to access millions of acres of government land and hunt rocks to your heart's content constitutes a paradise, then Nevada qualifies. If you think that being able to enjoy your hobby in uncrowded conditions is the definition of paradise, then Nevada certainly qualifies. (According to the U.S. Census Bureau, Lincoln County encompasses 10,633.61 square miles, but has only 0.4 persons per square mile. To put this in perspective, Bristol County, Rhode Island, encompasses only 24.68 square miles but has 2,025.9 persons for each of those square miles.) Finally, if you agree that being able to find agate, opal, jasper, fossils, fluorescent minerals, obsidian, chalcedony, wonderstone, malachite, petrified wood, limb casts, and much more means paradise, then you should stop reading right now and head for Nevada. It surely is a rockhound's paradise.

In case you haven't left yet, just listen to some of the statistics of this unique state. Nevada covers 110,000 square miles or 70,288,634 acres. This makes it the seventh largest state in the nation. Even more impressive to the rockhound is the fact that of those more than 70 million acres, nearly 60 million are owned by the federal government. Almost 50 million acres are run by the Bureau of Land Management (BLM), and that means plenty of rockhounding.

It also means an uncrowded state. If you like that uncrowded feeling, think about this. If you were to remove the population and land of the Las Vegas and Reno areas, the crowding factor would become 0.008 of a person per acre, or 5.08 people per square mile. Contrast that with some major cities, where it seems as though 200 people fight for the same parking place every day.

In the distant past, not only were there fewer people per square mile, there were, of course, no people at all. In fact, most of what is now Nevada was underwater and was the domain of the ichthyosaur, a late-Triassic marine reptile that grew to lengths of up to 60 feet. Through the intervening millions of years, the wiggling and squirming caused by plate tectonics caused the land to tilt upward and the water to flow westward. Eventually, what had been a continental shelf a few miles from the coastline became humid coastal marshes and swamps,

This view will greet you as you look across the lower sump from the upper sump.

then high mountains and high, lush valleys. In the next phase, ice from the last ice age covered much of the land. As the ice slowly melted, the water gathered in depressions and created a huge body of water known as Lake Lahontan. The draining and drying continued, and today only Pyramid and Walker Lakes remain as testament to a body of water that once covered most of the state.

What was once the bottom of a warm, shallow sea is now a high-altitude bowl that reaches from the Sierras to Salt Lake City and from Oregon to Death Valley. Aptly named the Great Basin, this bowl gets all of its water from the rivers fed by snowmelt in the mountains. No water flows out of the Great Basin in any direction. Roughly in the center of this bowl, Nevada is the driest state in the nation. Considering all of the activity that turned an ocean bottom into a high desert, it may be fitting that the state fossil of Nevada is one of those huge marine reptiles, the ichthyosaur.

The massive geological activity that created present-day Nevada did more than just fossilize the ichthyosaur, though. It created huge deposits of gold, silver, and many other minerals essential to the existence of modern man. The frenzied activity that wrested these treasures from the earth had a secondary benefit. It gave us rockhounds countless tailings piles and mine dumps upon which to practice our hobby.

The almost incomprehensible forces that made this great state created the mineral wonders we seek. Grab the rock bags and hammers, get in the car, and head for a rockhound's paradise. Nevada is waiting.

Finding Your Way

I have made every effort to provide accurate maps with usable landmarks and all available highway and road designations. Many of the sites in this book are in very remote areas and, obviously, there are no road names or street signs. Even though there will often be designations on various government and commercial maps, there are seldom matching signs along the gravel and dirt roads and four-wheel-drive tracks. Wherever there was a sign, I have included it in the text and on the map. The mileages given in the text are as accurate as the odometer on my vehicle. The major problem, of course, is that even on freeways odometer readings will vary, and on jeep roads where the wheels are constantly bouncing, they are notoriously bad. Thus, the mileage figures must be taken as approximate. Whenever possible, I have included prominent and reasonably permanent landmarks. Standard highway maps are a help in getting you to the point where my maps start. USGS topographic maps are indispensable for hikers, but for rockhounding purposes are not very helpful because they do not usually show most of the kinds of roads rockhounds use, and the ones they show are often very inaccurate.

Because most old dirt roads and tracks were built to get to a specific destination that has long since been abandoned, these roads may deteriorate due to lack of maintenance, but generally still go to the original destination. Possibly the biggest problem in finding the way to a site is caused by the seemingly constant activity of humans, even in these remote areas. New roads, tracks, trails, junctions, and forks spring up all the time and make following maps difficult (and in some cases, impossible). Technology has come to the rescue, though. Global positioning systems (GPS) almost make maps irrelevant. With just a small, hand-held unit—or the GPS in your vehicle—and the coordinates

I have provided in this edition, you can find your target site regardless of how many new forks in the road show up. It doesn't matter whether the roads are shown on the map in your GPS unit or not, since in most cases the unit will point you to the correct fork. Even if you do take the wrong one, the unit will show that you are moving away from your route and you can make the correction before you have gone miles off course.

Maybe the most important feature of GPS is one that doesn't get mentioned enough. It will also get you back to your starting point. When you are returning and you come to a three-way fork, do you remember which one you came in on? I know that I rarely do. The GPS does, though, and it will get you safely back to your starting point.

It is very easy to get lost in some of these remote areas, and this can be not just inconvenient, but disastrous as well. Since GPS coordinates for each site have been provided in this guide, I cannot urge you strongly enough to buy or borrow a GPS unit and take advantage of the coordinates when visiting any of the remote sites in this book.

I have also done my best to indicate the type of vehicle necessary to get to all of the sites. On some roads the family sedan is fine, but most of the time a high-clearance vehicle is needed. And for some spots, a four-wheel-drive is absolutely necessary. Remember that the time of year you visit and the length of time since the road was maintained can change a road from one suitable for the family car to one requiring four-wheel-drive. Nevada is a wide-open place, and driving distances are often long and lonely. Make sure you have the right type of vehicle before you start. If you have any doubts about your vehicle or the place you are heading, inquire locally about road conditions and the site location before you start.

Have a Safe Trip

The rockhounding sites in this book are found both in the mountains and in the desert. Consequently, it is important for anyone venturing into these areas to be aware of the special rules of safety for these environments. I assume that all rockhounds know the simple rules of outdoor safety, so no attempt will be made to lecture on such things as wearing goggles, wearing hats in the summer, or using sunscreen. There are a few precautions you must take in the mountains and in the desert that can mean the difference between an enjoyable trip and a miserable one. In some cases, failure to follow the proper precautions can even mean the difference between life and death. If you are an experienced mountain and desert driver and rockhound, you can skip this section, but if you are new to these areas, take a minute to absorb the information in this discussion of things to watch out for. You may avoid a ruined trip or serious injury.

Except for the obvious, having a safe trip is divided into four general categories: mountain safety, desert safety, driving safety, and weather safety. Often, of course, the four are interrelated.

Mountain Safety

Just the word *mountain* brings to mind cliffs, peaks, drop-offs, and generally dangerous places. These can all be present, but danger need not be a part of them if some simple precautions are taken.

First, be sure you are in shape for the altitude at the site you will be visiting. The mountains in Nevada are not the 12,000- and 13,000-foot monsters of Colorado, but if you live at or near sea level and go to 6,000 feet or so, be sure that your brain tells your body what it is in for. Hiking, climbing, and scrambling up and down tailings piles or quarry walls can put a severe strain on your cardiovascular system, especially at these altitudes, so proceed with caution.

If you experience nausea or shortness of breath (warning signs of altitude sickness) get to a lower altitude as soon as possible.

If you are in a particularly rough or remote area, plan to be out by dark or have camping gear, food, and water with you. Remember, if the road looked rough or had some steep drop-offs on the way in, think about what it will be like in the dark.

Many old quarries are flooded. Be extremely careful around them. It is difficult to tell how deep the water may be, and the walls are often too steep to climb if you should fall in.

Tailings piles around old mines are often very slippery and unstable. You could slide a long way. Even if you should take such a slide and not be hurt, think about the climb back up.

Finally, although it seems obvious, wear proper footwear. In the mountains, you will be walking over lots of rocks (not the kind you want to pick up and take home), and it is easy to sprain an ankle.

Desert Safety

Probably the most important safety rule for the desert explorer is to go in pairs or groups. If you have to go alone, let someone know your destination and expected time of your return. Only the most dyed-in-the-wool (crazy) rockhounds venture into the desert in the summer months. If you are one of those, be sure you leave a will or living trust.

Even in the winter months the desert can be an unforgiving place. Be sure you have plenty of water and an emergency supply of canned or dried food.

Canned is better, because it contains water. Dried food uses up your precious supply of water.

Beware of critters. Because of the daytime heat, most desert-dwelling critters are nocturnal. Since you probably won't be rockhounding at night, you may never see some of them. Snakes are a big worry to many people, but most have a rather narrow band of temperature in which they can function. Too hot and they are dead; too cold and they are immobile. Somewhere in between and they can gitcha.

There are some myths about rattlers that you should be aware of. The first is that old picture in some minds of rattlesnakes sunning themselves on a hot rock. In the heat of a desert day, if you see a rattler on a hot rock, it is either a belt or a hatband (or dead). The second is that, unlike the snakes in those sci-fi movies, snakes do not follow people and attack them. Snakes deserve much more credit. If you saw something about a bazillion times bigger than yourself, would you run up to it and punch it? What would a snake do with you? He can't eat you. He can't make a belt or a hatband out of you. Besides, he's afraid of you. Now, this in no way means that you should just assume everything is okay and you can forget about snakes. You absolutely cannot. Snakes do not like the direct heat of the sun, so in the daytime they are usually in holes, under logs, or in rock piles. The best advice, then, is not to put your hands or feet where you cannot see them.

Scorpions can be nasty little critters, too. They also are nocturnal, so use the same precautions as with snakes. If you camp out, be sure to check your boots in the morning before putting them on. Scorpions are notorious for hiding in boots. This advice, if followed, will make it possible to have a very safe desert trip. In fact, you may go for years and seldom, if ever, encounter a snake or scorpion.

There are some man-made hazards in the desert, too. Old mines are always dangerous, but the desert mines are especially so. Unlike the hardrock mines in the mountains, desert mines are often dug in sand and shored up with timbers. As the timbers rot away, the mine becomes a big hollow bubble under the ground. Cave-ins are common where the miners dug too close to the surface. Don't ever go in an old mine, and be extremely careful when walking around desert mines. There are often unmarked shafts, and there is the ever-present danger of a cave-in.

Driving Safety in the Mountains

Many, if not most, old mine roads and jeep roads are one lane with only occasional pullouts for passing. If you drive roads like this for long, you will, sooner or later, meet another vehicle going the opposite way, and there will be no pullout. This is one of those situations that we all dread, but they will happen, and it is important to know just how to handle them when they do.

Remember the most important rule: **The vehicle traveling uphill has the right of way.** It is much more dangerous to try to back down a hill than up one. This is hard to understand sometimes, but it is easy for a vehicle backing down to get going too fast and get out of control.

While the best method is to do everything you can to avoid confronting another vehicle head on, it will probably happen. In order to make the situation as panic-free as possible, keep a few things in mind as you drive along. First, try to remember where the turnouts are if you can. It will help your peace of mind if you have to back up to one. Second, keep an eye out for approaching vehicles as far ahead as you can. Even though you may be going uphill, if you see a vehicle coming and you can pull over near where you are, you may prevent a confrontation. Unfortunately, not all drivers use this courtesy and will just keep coming as though the road will suddenly widen out. Finally, don't panic, and don't try to pass the other vehicle or let it pass you unless you are 100 percent certain that it is safe to do so. I have seen vehicles try to pass by driving onto the cut slope (uphill bank) and tipping dangerously. I have also seen them go perilously close to the fill slope. Just stay calm, and if you are the vehicle going downhill, back up slowly and carefully. Remember, the rocks will wait.

It is certainly not a crime to be a novice when it comes to back-road mountain driving, but it may well be a crime not to admit it. There will be times when you crest a hill and see only sky in front of you. The road drops down, but you cannot see it over the hood. The novice who thinks he is a pro will drive on, betting that the road is really there and that it doesn't take a sharp turn. The sensible driver will stop and have a passenger get out and take a look, or he will stop the engine, block a wheel with a convenient rock, and take a look himself. Doing this may seem "sissy" or too time-consuming, but it can prevent an accident or even death.

Many back country roads such as shelf roads, narrow roads with no room for passing or turnaround, and roads that come to a dead end without warning (some with dangerous or even deadly drop offs) can pose problems as well. There is a shelf road up behind the Aspen Mine in Colorado that looks all right as it begins, but it rounds a blind curve and ends at a washout. It is barely one lane, and the drop-off is hundreds of feet. If you've ever had to back out of a situation like this, you won't want to repeat it. If you're not sure you can turn around on a road, get out and walk a ways. It will save you time, embarrassment, and possible serious injury. The bottom line in this kind of driving is this: If you aren't sure of the road condition, find out. If you can't find out, don't go.

Driving Safety in Deserts

In driving safety as in general desert safety, the primary rule is don't go alone if you can help it. If you must go alone, be sure that someone knows where you are going and your estimated time of return.

The big culprit in desert driving is sand. To avoid problems, first be sure you have a vehicle that can handle sandy roads. I will tell you the conditions at each site, but conditions can change, so you should always be on the lookout for problem areas.

If you do much desert driving, sooner or later you will get stuck in sand. Even the best of the four-wheel drives can end up in this unhappy situation, so don't buy a disguise and change your name if it happens to you. Be prepared and know what to do, and you will come out of it intact.

Be sure to have a good shovel with you. A full-size model is best, but if space is a problem, one of those little folding jobs will do. A tow strap is a good idea, too. If there is another vehicle in the party, you may get pulled out. Again, if you have the space, a nice little pile of old boards can be a lifesaver. Another nice accessory is a small air compressor. You can do without it, but if you have room, take one. Finally, have a good jack. This will probably not be the one that the factory put in your vehicle. The best way to find one is to go to a local off-road store and talk to the folks. Different types of jacks work better with certain vehicles, so talk to the experts before you buy.

The best way to avoid getting stuck is to know what you are driving on. If the stretch ahead looks sandy or suspicious, get out and walk it. It may be macho to plow ahead, but macho can cost you a lot of time and labor. If you find yourself in soft sand, keep going. If you stop, the chances are you will not get started again. Instead, your wheels will just dig a hole.

When your forward progress stops, get off the gas pedal and put the transmission in neutral. Climb out and assess the situation. Your first decision will be to determine which way to go. If you just entered the sandy area and the road ahead looks bad, you may want to back out. On the other hand, the situation may be just the reverse. When you have decided which way to go, get out your shovel and start moving sand away from the wheels in the direction you want to go. If you brought boards along, put them ahead of the wheels. Get back in the vehicle and **ease** it forward (or backward). If you get going, try to keep it going. Keep a soft foot on the throttle. If you give it too much gas, your wheels will dig another hole.

If you can't get it moving, try jacking the wheels up one at a time and put your boards or some branches or rocks—anything you can find—under the wheels. This may get you going. If nothing else works, try letting about half of the air out of the tires. This will make a broader footprint, allowing you to "float" over the top of the sand.

Weather Safety in the Mountains

The weather can be a real problem for driving anywhere, but on a remote jeep road it can be much worse. Note the kind of surface of the road as you go along. Nevada may be extremely dry, but it does rain, and there are areas where snow can be a problem too. A road surface that looks like friendly dirt can become so slick in the rain that you might rather have ice. Old mine roads are given minimal maintenance at best, and a rain that doesn't look too bad can cause washouts that will be impassable. If you are in a remote area and rain is impending, think about the road you drove there on. Maybe you should pack up and leave. Remember, also, that with rain often come thunder and lightning. If either is present, seek shelter as fast as possible. If no other shelter is available and your vehicle has a steel top, get in and don't touch the steering wheel or any other metal parts. There is an old myth that the rubber tires insulate a vehicle from the ground. Not so. A lightning strike would follow the metal skin of the vehicle and either jump to ground or follow a path across the wet surface of the tires. Of course, the best way to avoid all of this is to get out at the first sign of a coming storm. I know well the feeling that your beautiful gemstone is just one or two more jabs away with the shovel, but no gemstone is worth playing tag with a lightning bolt and losing. There will always be another day to hunt, and it might be a long walk out if the road should wash out and even worse if that lightning bolt should catch you.

Don't let all of these gloomy prospects deter you from the fun of rock-hounding in the mountains, but do practice good old horse sense. It will make your experience one to look back on with pleasure.

Weather Safety in Deserts

When most people think of desert weather, they think of hot summer sun and maybe some wind. These happen, of course, but so do rainstorms and flash floods. In Nevada, most of the rockhound sites are in desert areas, but many are close to mountains. The most fearsome thing to have happen is to see a wall of muddy water come crashing down a "dry" creek bed (known in the West as a wash) in the middle of a bright sunny day. The rain may have fallen miles away in the mountains, but the water ends up in washes way out on the desert. If you were unfortunate enough to be in such a wash at the time of a flash flood, you would be lucky to survive.

Never camp in a wash. These wide washes look like great camping spots, and may provide some shade and shelter from the wind, but they can become raging rivers at a moment's notice. This is also something to think about when driving. Do you have an alternate route out in case a wash floods? Lightning can be an even more dangerous problem on the flat desert than in the mountains, so please follow the previous section's suggestions. Remember that in the desert you are often the highest point on the landscape and, as such, are in effect a lightning rod.

The nice part about flash floods in the desert is that in many cases, in an hour or so, the wash will be dried up and look as though there had been no water in it in a hundred years.

As with the mountains, a little horse sense goes a long way in tackling desert weather. Wear a hat, wear sunglasses, use sunscreen, and wear loose-fitting clothes and shirts with long sleeves. And have lots of water.

Abandoned Mine Safety

The dangers that exist around abandoned mines would appear to be obvious, but many people just seem to forget. They forget, for example, that falling down some of the old deep shafts would be similar to falling off a tall building. Because the distance is not readily visible, the danger is masked. All shafts, portals, and drifts should be avoided.

Many of the old mines have been left to the elements for nearly a hundred years, and the shoring has probably rotted away. It is also well to remember that the engineering in many of the mines was often hit or miss to begin with, so that many of the mines may not have been safe when they were originally opened up. The best advice is never to enter an abandoned mine. Decayed timbers and open shafts are only two of the many hazards.

Many of the old mines are wet, and pools can sometimes be deceptively deep. It is not unheard of for someone to drown in a mine. Bad air is another possibility. Suffocation is not worth the pursuit of anything the mountain may have to offer. One thought should keep any sane person out of such danger. If there were riches worth risking life or limb for down in the depths, then why was the place abandoned?

As I was writing this book, an article appeared in our local paper about two men who died of suffocation in an abandoned Nevada mine. The mine had a warning posted cautioning people to stay out due to bad air. These signs are not to be treated frivolously.

Children, of course, must be watched constantly. Naturally, they have to be kept away from the underground workings, but there are many more kinds of trouble that they can get into. Many of the sites listed in this guide—and virtually all of the mines—are on very steep mountainsides. In addition, tailings piles are steep and often unstable. While it might not be fatal, a slide down a

This is just one of the many strange formations in the lower sump area (Site 79).

large pile could result in broken bones and other serious injuries a long way from medical help.

All of this gloom is not meant to keep the reader from exploring these fascinating spots for fear of some disaster awaiting. There is no reason why such exploration cannot be safe and pleasurable. A good dose of caution and common sense will ensure that it will be.

Happy hunting.

Rockhound Etiquette

Although it should be obvious, it is an often overlooked fact that all land belongs to somebody. Those of us cursed with living in a city have no trouble with this concept. We don't question the fact that even the rare vacant lot is not available for public use. But when we get out into the wide open spaces, we sometimes forget that just because there is nothing on the land, and there are no KEEP OUT signs, permission to enter is not given automatically. Every square inch of the United States belongs to somebody.

Nevada, for example, covers a total of approximately 70,288,634 acres. The federal government owns approximately 60,863,345 acres, about 1,136,458 acres are privately owned, 158,116 acres are tribal lands, and the balance is owned by the state and localities. Each private owner makes his own rules for rock collecting, and each governmental agency does the same. If we are to be responsible rockhounds and keep the lands available to us, we need to know and follow each entity's rules and regulations.

Unwritten Rules

It is sometimes hard to remember, especially when hunting around some of the old mining areas, that we should try as much as humanly possible to leave the land looking as though we had not been there. If you do a lot of digging, fill in the holes before you leave. Don't dismantle old buildings, even if you want to make picture frames or a coffee table with that beautiful weathered wood. Always leave gates as you find them. If the gate was closed, close it behind you. If it was open, even though it may seem wrong, leave it open. It should go without saying that you should take out any trash you brought in, and it won't hurt if you take any that someone else may have left. The cleaner we keep these sites, the better the chance that they will stay open.

Bureau of Land Management

The BLM defines a rockhound as one who collects rocks, minerals, and fossils as a hobby. As such, rockhounding is permitted on all of BLM lands with a few restrictions.

First, the rockhound must not create a significant disturbance. This is a bit vague, but common sense tells us that you should not dig to the point where you cause erosion of the land or pollution of streams or other water sources. Nor should you drive your vehicle on soft soil where the wheel tracks will create gullies and promote erosion.

Small amounts of rock and mineral specimens are allowed to be collected, but "small" is an undefined term. The rules are to differentiate between recreational collectors and commercial miners, so it seems that if you can lift your rock bag and carry it to your vehicle, you are probably okay.

Fossil collecting has some special regulations. Except in designated areas, plant and invertebrate fossils may be collected without restriction. Vertebrate fossils (fish, mammals) may not be collected on BLM lands.

If you would like the latest information on the collecting status of various areas, or could use some directions or maps, drop in to or call the local BLM office. The addresses and phone numbers are in Appendix A.

USDA Forest Service

Forest service rules and regulations for minerals and fossils are essentially the same as those of the BLM.

Private Property

I cannot overemphasize the importance of getting permission before collecting on private property. Owners of farms and ranches are usually very good about allowing those who ask to collect on their property if it will not interfere with their operations. However, in the wide, open spaces it's sometimes difficult to find out just who owns the land. The only way to gain access to such spots is to go to the county recorder's office and try to find a name and address for the owner. This is a time-consuming process, but if the site looks particularly good, it might be worth the effort. Please, though, resist the urge to enter the land just because there is no one watching.

In the case of mines on public lands, it is reasonable to assume that if there is no posting and no sign of recent work, it is probably okay to collect on the tailings piles. But it is never a good idea to enter the mine. There is a small group of "miners" who feel that putting a sign of any kind on a rock site guarantees them access to half of the western United States. If you think that this is the case, check it out at the local forest service or BLM office.

Where Collecting Is Prohibited

Collecting is not allowed in national parks, state parks, or national monuments, although many parks have interesting rockhound-related displays. The best rule of thumb for determining a property's collecting status is to ask the owner— whether that is a private landowner or a government agency.

Fluorescence and the Rockhound

Most rockhounds have seen displays of fluorescent minerals at rock and gem shows. But I suspect that, like me, they thought that these were all exotic, rare, and expensive minerals, and that to gather them and buy a "black light" would cost a king's ransom. Actually a lot of very common rocks will fluoresce very well, and small, handheld ultraviolet lamps with both long- and shortwave bulbs can be bought for a modest sum.

Of course, as with gear for so many other hobbies, the larger units can cost many hundreds of dollars, but they are not necessary for you to enjoy watching a rock you carried home glow in the amazing colors that fluorescence offers. Several of the sites in this book list chalcedonies and calcites that fluoresce well and are very common. Some of the little warty-looking chalcedonies would not even be carried home if it were not for their fluorescent qualities.

The downside of this is that you cannot tell by looking at a sample in daylight whether it will fluoresce or not. Consequently, you have the choice of taking a small, battery-operated lamp along to identify samples or to haul home a whole lot of useless bits of ugly rock. The answer is to take your lamp along and make a darkroom out of a jacket or sweater in order to view the sample in near darkness. Of course, on a bright day, this is hard to do, but I find that I can usually get it dark enough to tell if the sample will fluoresce. Then at home I can get the full beauty in total darkness.

Fluorescence is a fascinating study and is part of a more general physical property of minerals known as luminescence. This property has some subproperties with tongue-twister names. "Phosphorescence" is the afterglow that remains in certain minerals when the ultraviolet light is turned off. "Thermoluminescence" is a glow produced in some minerals when they are reheated. "Triboluminescence" is light produced by striking, crushing, or scratching certain minerals. "Cathodoluminescence" is luminescence produced by striking certain minerals with an electron beam. And, of course, "fluorescence" is color produced in certain minerals by flooding them with ultraviolet light.

There are many wavelengths of ultraviolet light, but the shortwave (approximately 254 nanometers) and long-wave (approximately 360 nanometers) are the most common for viewing rocks and minerals. Some will fluoresce under one wavelength and not the other, and some will fluoresce under both. For the hobbyist, the most practical lamp is one with tubes of both wavelengths. This is particularly true in the field, where a good sample might be missed because the wrong wavelength of light was used to test it.

The study of fluorescence involves some serious science, but all the hobbyist needs is a desire to see some beautiful colors, a simple ultraviolet lamp, and some samples of minerals that are easily collected or even bought. You can buy the lamps at many rock shops or mining supply dealers. If you cannot find one locally, contact one of the following:

UVP Incorporated
2066 West 11th St.
Upland, CA 91786
(909) 946-3597
(800) 452-6788
fax: (909) 946-3597
uvp@uvp.com
www.uvp.com

Excalibur Mineral Corporation
1000 North Division St.
Peekskill, NY 10566
(914) 739-1134
fax: (914) 739-1257
www.excaliburmineral.com

Raytech
475 Smith St.
Middletown, CT 06457
(860) 632-2020
fax: (860) 632-1699
www.raytech-ind.com

Sights along the Way

As you travel throughout Nevada visiting the rockhounding sites in this book, you will pass by many fascinating points of interest. Many of these are state and national parks where rock collecting is not permitted, but they are of great interest to most rockhounds anyway. It is also possible, when talking to the rangers and other park employees, to get some good information on legal collecting sites.

Berlin-Ichthyosaur State Park

The name of this park is quite a mouthful, but you do get two for the price of one when you visit. The park gets its name from the ghost town of Berlin and the giant prehistoric sea creatures called ichthyosaurs, which swam in the ancient sea in the neighborhood of 225 million years ago. The ichthyosaurs disappeared with the vanishing sea, and the miners disappeared with the vanishing gold and silver.

At the park you can tour the well-preserved ghost town and view a partially excavated dig containing the fossilized remains of nine ichthyosaurs that have been left in the rock in their original positions. This is unusual since, although ichthyosaurs are not rare, most displays are of remains that have been removed from the dig and placed in a museum setting. The park is open from Memorial Day to Labor Day. Because of the 7,000-foot altitude, winter often covers the park with snow.

If you visit Sites 61 or 62, or if you try the Gabbs Trip in the "Intrepid Explorer" section, you just might want to stop by and visit this unique park. Another plus is the nice campground with biking and hiking trails.

Finding the park: Go east on NV 844 from its junction with NV 361 just north of Gabbs. Follow NV 844 for about 18 miles to the park entrance.

For more information: Berlin-Ichthyosaur State Park; NV 844, Gabbs, NV 89310; (775) 964-2440; http://parks.nv.gov/bi.htm.

Cathedral Gorge State Park

If you are poking around the sites at Pioche, be sure to take a run over to Cathedral Gorge State Park. This is one of Nevada's lesser known, but more beautiful, sights. Roughly a million years ago, this whole valley was covered by a lake. Streams in the area washed silt containing various minerals from the surrounding hills into the lake, where it settled on the bottom forming a 1,500-foot thick crust. Faults in the mountains at the southern end of the lake allowed the water to drain slowly away. In the process, it carved the deep canyon, with colorful formations and little caves along the fault line. After the lake finally dried up, those willing forces of nature—sun, wind, and rain—continued the work of carving and shaping the gorge into the amazing sight it is today. The park covers 1,633 acres, including a campground, picnic area, and hiking trails.

Finding the site: From the junction of US 93 and NV 319 near Panaca, drive north on US 93 for 2 miles to the park entrance.

For more information: Cathedral Gorge State Park, P.O. Box 176, Panaca, NV 89042; (777) 728-4460; http://parks.nv.gov/cg.htm.

Death Valley National Park

Although nearly all of Death Valley National Park lies within California and not Nevada, it is right on the border, and it wouldn't be against the law to slip across under cover of darkness and do a little exploring. At the very least you should go over and see Scotty's Castle, since you will be on the road to that unique spot if you are picking up obsidian or the beautifully detailed pumice/wood at Scotty's Junction. If you have never seen the castle, it is a must. It is one of those things that everyone should experience at least once in a lifetime—like the Statue of Liberty, Washington D.C., Paris in the spring, and an IRS audit.

Although it is known as "Scotty's Castle," this architectural wonder was actually the brainchild and property of Albert Johnson, an insurance company executive from Chicago. He and Scotty, who was actually a prospector named Walter Scott, first met in Chicago when Scott approached Johnson about forming a partnership in a gold venture in the desert. (There are those who define Scotty's prospecting proposal a little differently. Their definition includes the suffix "con.") The two became lifelong friends and spent many winters roaming the desert in search of gold.

They never found any, but Johnson did find health, peace, and happiness. Consequently, he began buying up property around Grapevine Canyon, a perfect spot with abundant water that, at an altitude of 3,000 feet, was out of the terrible heat of the valley but not high enough for the winter cold and snow of the high Nevada basin. In 1922, the first buildings were built, and by 1925, the "castle" was starting to take shape.

Because of the Great Depression of the 1930s, however, the project was never completed. A substantial amount of it was, though, and today you can visit the twenty-five-room mansion, which is filled with beautiful furnishings and valuable artwork, and the nine surrounding buildings. This compound would be impressive if it were in Beverly Hills, but sitting on the edge of one of the most inhospitable places on Earth and miles from anything, it is a sight to behold and one I hope you don't miss.

Finding the site: To reach the castle, turn southwest on NV 267 at its junction with US 95, about 36 miles north of Beatty. Follow NV 267 for about 20 miles to the castle entrance.

For more information: Death Valley National Park, P.O. Box 579, Death Valley, CA 92328; (760) 786-3200; http://www.nps.gov/deva/index.htm.

Fort Churchill State Historic Park

The Weeks and Old Highway sites are just a stone's throw from Fort Churchill State Historic Park. This 710-acre park was the site of the first and the largest army base built after the Pyramid Lake War, originally covering 1,400 acres. The fort was built in 1860 and was intended to protect miners in the rapidly expanding mining camps and travelers on the Overland Route. For a short time, it was a Pony Express station and a telegraph station. When the transcontinental railway was completed, the fort was declared obsolete, and in 1871 it was sold at auction for $750.

After the sale, the fort served for a time as an Indian school, but most of the time, until the 1930s, it was just used as a storage facility for construction materials. Eventually, the National Park Service did a little restoration work, and the Civilian Conservation Corps built a visitor center. In 1957, Fort Churchill became a Nevada state park.

Today, the park has displays of the Pony Express, the telegraph, and the Pyramid Lake War. In addition, there is a small campground and a walking trail down to the ruins of the fort.

Finding the park: Drive south from Silver Springs on US 95 for about 8 miles to the well-marked gravel road leading west 1 mile to the park.

For more information: Fort Churchill State Historic Park, 10000 US 95A, Silver Springs, NV 89429; (775) 577-2345; http://parks.nv.gov/fc.htm.

Great Basin National Park

Great Basin National Park covers 77,100 acres just east of Ely and ranges from a low altitude of 6,200 feet at Snake Creek to 13,068 feet at Wheeler Peak. If you are rockhounding around the Major's Place or Garnet Hill sites, or if you are heading over into Utah, by all means stop a while and look over this fascinating place.

As national parks go, Great Basin is small. It is also remote. The largest town, Ely, is 70 miles away. This tends to reduce the urban atmosphere that permeates so many parks. People who come to Great Basin tend to be there for the beauty and tranquility rather than just to put another park notch on their itineraries.

The park is comprised of Lehman Caves and a large chunk of the Humboldt National Forest. Although this area was proposed as a national park in 1922, when Lehman Caves became a national monument, the powerful ranching and mining interests in the area had no use for a national park messing up their fun. It was not until October 1986 that Nevada's only national park came into being.

Although there is much to do in the park if you like to hike or just commune with nature, the two most visited areas are probably Lehman Caves and the bristlecone pine forest. Although referred to as Lehman Caves, there is actually just one cave. The cave was discovered by Absalom Lehman, a rancher and miner, around 1885. It's small by cave standards; it only extends into the limestone and marble about 0.25 mile, but it is one of the most beautifully decorated to be found anywhere. Besides the usual stalactites, stalagmites, draperies, flowstone, and columns, there are some rare formations. One of these is a formation called shields. These occur in halves much like flattened clam shells. Their formation is still a mystery to science.

Not a mystery but still a wonder are the great bristlecone pines. Clinging to life for thousands of years at 11,000 feet, they have endured freezing cold, high winds, poor soil, and a generally poor growing environment since long before Christ's time. One bristlecone here was dated at almost 5,000 years old. A good trail leads to the bristlecone forest, and you just have to give it a try. Think how your flatland neighbors will gaze at you with awe as you tell them stories of your journey.

Finding the park: Drive east from Ely on US 93/50/6 for about 27 miles, to the junction at Major's Place. At this point, US 50 and US 6 head east, and US 93 goes south. Take US 50/6 east for another 35 miles or so to Baker. At Baker, take NV 488 to the park.

For more information: Great Basin National Park, 100 Great Basin National Park, Baker, NV 89311-9700; (775) 234-7331; http://www.nps.gov/grba/index.htm

Hoover Dam

Hoover Dam is another of those sights that is almost mandatory for everyone to see at least once. If you are in the Las Vegas area and have never been to the dam, be sure to go. The statistics surrounding this wonder are mind-boggling in themselves, but the sight of the dam, both inside and out, is one you will never forget.

The idea for the dam came after the disastrously wet winter and spring of 1905. Farmers in California's Imperial Valley had diverted water from the Colorado River to irrigate their fields for years, but in this year, flash floods changed the course of the Colorado. As it flowed through the valley, it changed the 22-square-mile puddle known as the Salton Sea into an inland sea of 500 square miles. It took engineers and farmers nearly two years to get the river back into its original channel. The message was clear—the Colorado had to be tamed.

After years of negotiating and haggling, a site was chosen for a dam, and in April 1931, work began on the Boulder Dam Project. The enormity of the project must have struck the first workers to arrive on the site as sheer insanity. Here was a huge canyon 40 miles out in the blistering heat of the desert from a sleepy little railroad town called Las Vegas. There were no roads, there were no railroads, and the nearest power plant of any size was in San Bernardino, more than 200 miles away. The Colorado had to be diverted around the proposed site. All of these things and much more would be needed before construction could begin.

Nevertheless, workers pressed forward and four tunnels, each 56 feet in diameter, were dug through the solid rock of the canyon walls. It took sixteen months of moving thousands of tons of rock, but in November 1932, the Colorado was diverted. For the next two years, tons of concrete were poured—seven million tons or 3.2 million cubic yards. At one point in the construction, 5,000 workers labored twenty-four hours a day to complete the dam. Over the forty-six months it took to complete the dam, there were an average of fifty accidents a day and a total of ninety-four deaths. Much of the construction equipment was the largest known in the world at that time, and most was built and installed on the site.

Today, you can tour this amazing structure year-round and see the giant turbines that generate four billion kilowatt-hours of electricity each year. You can stand at the foot and look up, in awe, 726 feet to the top of the dam. I'll bet you can even buy a T-shirt.

Finding the site: To reach Hoover Dam, drive south from Las Vegas on US 93 to Boulder City and follow the signs to the visitor center.

For more information: (702) 494-2517; www.usbr.gov/lc/hooverdam/service/index.html

Jarbidge

Way back before the turn of the twentieth century, prospectors had been wandering around the Jarbidge Mountains looking for the Lost Sheepherder's Ledge, one of the many lost sources of Western gold-hunting lore's untold riches. As the story goes, a sheepherder found a rich ledge of gold, but died before he could work it or even tell anyone about it. It may not have been the Lost Sheepherder, but in 1909, a prospector by the name of Bourne found gold just south of the present site of Jarbidge. In just two years, 1,500 hardy souls had converted the remote and wild area into a mining boom town. Today, Jarbidge may be best known as the place where the last stagecoach robbery in the United States took place. The driver was shot and several thousand dollars of miners' payroll money was never recovered.

In 1919 that scourge of all of the early Western towns—fire—destroyed much of Jarbidge, but within a year its not-to-be-denied citizens had rebuilt the area and turned Jarbidge into the state's largest gold producer. Many millions of dollars in gold were removed from the grip of the mountains by the 1930s.

Gold is only a memory for the few folks who call Jarbidge home today. It may well be one of the most remote towns in the West that still claims permanent residents. Two roads come up into the area from the Nevada side. Both are dirt, and each is more than 50 miles from pavement. Both are closed by snow for up to eight months of the year. One road goes north into Idaho and is only dirt for 18 miles. Unfortunately, it is still another 50 miles to town. The good news is that this road is kept open during the winter. Supplies are available in Twin Falls, Idaho, a short 100 miles away. If you are looking for a spot off the beaten track, I think this may be it.

As far off the beaten track as it is, however, lots of tourists find their way here every year. It is a beautiful spot. It is peaceful, and it is unique. Pick a nice warm summer day and join the other tourists. Remember, you can find some nice fossil leaves along the way at Copper Basin.

Finding the site: From the intersection of I-80 and NV 225 in Elko, go north on NV 225 for 53.4 miles to a road heading east and well marked with a sign indicating that it is the way to Jarbidge. Take this road east for 21 miles to a fork. Go left at the fork, then travel 6.4 miles to another fork. Take the road to the right and travel 6.9 miles, after which you will see a rough track going to the left. This track goes to the Copper Basin fossil site (Site 56). Keep on the main road for approximately 10 more miles to Jarbidge.

Lake Tahoe

No journey into northwestern Nevada for any purpose would be complete without a side trip to the crown jewel of mountain lakes—Tahoe. Even the jamming of condominiums, casinos, and neon signs into a place of unsurpassed natural splendor cannot blot out the deep blue beauty of "big water."

Nestled in a valley between the Sierra Nevada and the Carson Range at an altitude of 6,229 feet, Lake Tahoe still lies 4,000 feet below most of the peaks surrounding it. If Tahoe's beauty is impressive, its statistics are equally so. The lake is 22 miles long and 12 miles wide. Its water is nearly as pure as distilled water, and is remarkably clear. It is said that you can see a dinner plate sitting 75 feet deep in the lake. The average depth of the lake is 989 feet, and the deepest point is 1,645 feet. The 122 million acre-feet of water contained in Tahoe would cover the entire state of California 14 inches deep. (There are those who think it should.)

Even the name, Tahoe, came about in a unique way. Explorer John C. Frémont wanted to name the lake Bonpland after a French explorer, and the governors of both California and Nevada agreed on the name Bigler after the third governor of California. However, the chief cartographer evidently didn't like either one, since he left the names off the map. He then consulted an expert in the Washoe Indian tongue and subsequently named the lake Tahoe, from the Washoe *Da Ow A Ga* (Edge of the Lake).

For 5,000 years or so, the Washoe Indians gathered at the northern end of the lake to load up on the abundant trout and generally enjoy the beauty of the place. Members of their neighboring tribe, the Paiutes, made a big mistake and drew a map of the area for Frémont in about 1844. Frémont and his party followed the Truckee River to the lake, and the word was out. It wasn't long before the fishing industry had nearly fished out the lake, and the logging industries had logged off 50,000 of the 51,000 acres of forest surrounding the lake.

About this same time, luxury hotels were sprouting up to serve the wealthy mine owners on the Comstock Lode. The first narrow-gauge railroad reached Tahoe in 1900, and the first automobile in 1905. By 1930, there were paved roads to the lake, and the door was really open to everyone.

And everyone has come. If you are in the area, you had better run over for a look before someone decides to pave over the lake to make a parking lot for the mall.

Finding the site: To reach the Lake Tahoe basin, travel a little more than 10 miles west of Carson City on US 50.

Pyramid Lake

Just a short 30 miles north of Sparks, surrounded by barren desert hills, is a turquoise jewel of a lake. Named for the strange rock formation that rises from its sparkling waters, Pyramid Lake is one of only two bodies of water in Nevada left by the receding of ancient Lake Lahontan. Pyramid is seen by some as the most beautiful desert lake in the world. It is also one of the largest freshwater lakes in the western United States, although at about 30 miles long and 7 to 9 miles wide, it is tiny in comparison to its ancestor, Lahontan, which covered 8,400 square miles.

In addition to its natural beauty, Pyramid is unique in that it is home to the endangered cui-ui, a fish species that is found in this lake only. Like Pyramid itself, this type of lake sucker is a holdover from Lake Lahontan and has been around for tens of thousands of years. The cui-ui reach as much as seven pounds and can live to be forty years old.

If you are in the area doing a little rockhounding at the Cold Springs Valley Road site, why not hop over and take a look at this natural wonder? You can't catch a cui-ui, but you can take a lot of pictures that will dazzle the guys at the pool hall and the ladies at the bridge club when you get home.

Finding the site: To reach Pyramid Lake, drive north from Sparks on NV 445 for about 33 miles to the south end of the lake. You can also drive north from Wadsworth on NV 447 to Nixon, then go left on NV 446 to the lake. The route out of Sparks can be a little hard to find, so why not gas up the car and crank up the GPS?

For more information: www.pyramidlake.us

Red Rock Canyon National Conservation Area

Drive west out of Las Vegas on Charleston Boulevard (NV 159), and as you pass the last of the building sprawl on both sides of the road, you will find it hard to believe that only a few miles behind you is the glitz and glitter capital of the Western world. Ahead, the road stretches toward the Spring Mountains, and right to Red Rock Canyon. To the sides of the road are Joshua trees and sand. If it were not for the blacktop highway, the scene could be from any time in the past 10,000 years. Behind are the glaring colors of neon, and ahead are the reds, grays, yellows, oranges, and purples of the ancient sandstone cliffs. I guess each has its place, but I'll take the sandstone.

The geologic formations in Red Rock Canyon show clearly how the area was formed. From the bottom of a huge inland sea, through faulting and upthrusting and the sculpting action of wind and rain, this beautiful area has almost mimicked the metamorphosis of the butterfly.

If you like to study the geology of an area, this is your place. If you just appreciate the amazing feats of nature, this is your place, too. In fact, if you like anything about the outdoor world, you are bound to find something to enjoy in the 196,000 acres of Red Rock Canyon National Conservation Area.

If you don't want to get far from the car, there is a 13-mile loop road with scenic overlooks and picnic sites. For the more hardy among you, there are numerous trails to hike, and for the lionhearted, there is rock climbing galore. This is another spot you must see if you are in the Las Vegas area. You might want to hurry, too, since Las Vegas is growing so fast that before long, Red Rock Canyon may be in the heart of downtown. Sort of a desert Central Park.

Finding the site: To reach Red Rock Canyon, drive west from Las Vegas on Charleston Boulevard (NV 159) for 20 miles. Turn at the well-marked visitor center.

For more information: Red Rock Canyon National Conservation Area, 4701 N. Torrey Pines Dr., Las Vegas, NV 89130; (702) 515-5000; www .redrockcanyonlv.org/index.html

Sheldon National Wildlife Refuge

If you head for any of the Virgin Valley fee-to-dig opal mines, you will drive right past the Dufurrena Field Station at the Sheldon National Wildlife Refuge. Why not stop in and gab with the rangers? Within the confines of the refuge, you will find golden eagles, prairie falcons, American kestrels, Canada geese, mallard ducks, killdeer, California quail, chukars, sage grouse, mule deer, and bighorn sheep. However, the real prize, and the reason most people come here, is the pronghorn antelope.

Pronghorns once bounced over the plains of the West by the millions, but the relentless westward movement of humankind, with its baggage of disease, overgrazing the grasslands, hunting, and even deliberate poisoning, reduced the herds to the point where they were near extinction. One small herd of pronghorns still roamed the northwest corner of Nevada, though, and in the early 1920s, the state director of predator control, Edward Sans, began a battle to provide a refuge for these beautiful animals. By 1938, 34,000 acres of ranchland had been purchased and set aside as a refuge for the pronghorns by President Herbert Hoover. The small refuge was named after Charles Sheldon, a hunter and writer who had maintained a long-term fascination and love for the animals. By 1937, additional land had been purchased and the refuge was expanded to its current 571,000 acres.

Finding the site: To reach the refuge from Winnemucca, go north on NV 140 for 96 miles to Denio Junction. At Denio Junction, stay on NV 140 for

25.1 miles, coming to the well-marked Virgin Valley turnoff. Turn onto the Virgin Valley Road and drive one mile to the Dufurrena Field Station. The Virgin Valley Campground is just one mile beyond the station.

For more information: Refuge Manager, Sheldon National Wildlife Refuge, P.O. Box 111, Lakeview, OR 97630; (503) 947-3315; www.fws.gov/refuges/profiles/index.cfm?id=84621

Valley of Fire State Park

The turnoff to Valley of Fire State Park, one of the West's premier red-rock areas, is a little over 30 miles north of Las Vegas on I-15. Similar in some respects to Red Rock Canyon, the 140-million-plus-year-old Mesozoic sandstone highlighted in this park is also found in Colorado, Utah, New Mexico, Arizona, and Nevada. Both the colors and the formations in Valley of Fire are truly spectacular. The colors range from scarlet through vermilion, mauve, gold, orange, burgundy, and magenta. The formations are a little harder to describe, but names like Elephant Rock, Limestone Hoodoos, Duck Rock, Cobra Rock, Grand Piano, and Beehive should give you some idea.

In addition to the formations, you can see petrified wood (no collecting), petroglyphs (old graffiti), and the breathtaking overlook at Rainbow Vista. Don't miss the visitor center. You can see a demonstration garden, a description of the geological history of the area (which dates back 550 million years), and displays of the history, ecology, and archaeology of the area.

Valley of Fire was originally part of the land set aside for the Boulder Dam Project in the 1920s. When the dam was finished and the land was no longer needed, it was given to Nevada for a state park. The state had no money for such activities in those days, so the federal government used the Civilian Conservation Corps to build some roads and campgrounds. In 1935, Valley of Fire was designated the first of Nevada's original four state parks. It is a jewel, so if you are in the area, don't miss it.

I will qualify my recommendation just a bit. If you are camping, try very hard to see the park in the spring or fall. The summer can be extremely hot, and the winter can be very cold. One year, when my sons were still in diapers, we camped in a tent here on the way to Christmas with grandpa and grandma in Utah. When we got the boys ready for bed, we put the wet diapers in a pan outside the tent so that we could take care of them in the morning. In the morning, however, they were frozen solid. (In fact, they didn't thaw out until late May.)

Finding the site: You can reach the Valley of Fire State Park in two ways. You can drive north from Las Vegas on I-15 for about 30 miles to the well-marked turnoff onto NV 169. From this junction, it is about 15 miles to the park entrance. If you are following NV 167 along Lake Mead from Boulder City, you can go about 50 miles to the junction of NV 169 at the eastern end of the park.

For more information: Valley of Fire State Park, 29450 Valley of Fire Rd., Overton, NV 89040; (702) 397-2088; http://parks.nv.gov/vf.htm

Virginia City

If you have even the smallest interest in the history of mining in the West, than you will have to see Virginia City. Once the biggest town on the Comstock Lode, and probably the biggest and most famous of all of the West's gold-mining towns, Virginia City saw the rise and fall of one of the greatest money-making machines in history.

When the gold rush began in California in the 1850s, the great wave of humanity with picks, shovels, and golden gleams in its eye washed right over Nevada and landed in the Sierra Nevada of California. As some of the hardy souls began to realize that they were not going to strike it rich there, the wave slowly began to flow back toward Nevada.

Some minor strikes east of Tahoe attracted the prospectors and miners. There was some luck, but much of the area was cursed with a blue sludge that clogged the sluice boxes and caused the miners no end of problems. They turned the air as blue as the sludge with their hatred of the stuff, until some wise soul realized that the terrible blue mud was actually very rich silver sulphurets. So rich was the muck that it assayed out at $875 per ton in gold and $3,000 per ton in silver.

Thus began the fabulous Comstock Lode, whose wealth flowed out in profusion to build much of San Francisco, help finance the Union Army in the Civil War, and build transcontinental railroads, undersea telegraph cables across the Atlantic, steamship lines, and palaces in Italy and France. Of course, it also made possible the development of Nevada in the nineteenth century and led to its statehood. The story of Virginia City is long and fascinating. If you are interested, you should pick up one of the many books written about it.

To visit the city today is to find yourself in a strange conglomeration of museums, historical buildings, motor homes, and every other kind of recreational vehicle. You will wander the old streets where Mark Twain and Bret Harte walked, and you will be sharing those streets with folks in cowboy hats and boots, young folks in hiking boots and with backpacks, and overfed tourists wearing Bermuda shorts and knee-length black socks. Tune out the weird and feel the history, and you will have a most enjoyable and educational experience.

Finding the site: If you have gathered all of the mineral specimens you need and have avoided the rattlesnakes at the Cold Springs Valley Road site, drive south on US 395 to the junction with NV 341. Go east on NV 341 for about 10 or 15 miles to Virginia City.

For more information: Virginia City Convention and Tourism Authority, 86 South C St., Virginia City, NV 89440; (800) 718-7587; www.virginiacity-nv.org

Ward Charcoal Ovens State Historic Park

If you have stopped at Garnet Hill, why not take a short side trip to the historic old charcoal ovens near the ghost town of Ward?

Back during the years from 1872 to 1882, Ward was a lawless mining camp of about 2,000 people. Accounts vary as to just how much silver was taken out of the Ward Mining District's mines. Figures range from as little as a quarter-million dollars to more than a million dollars from one mine alone. Whatever it was, it is all but forgotten now.

Today, the draw is the six beautifully built beehive-shaped brick ovens, or kilns, which were used to make charcoal for the smelter. Each oven is 30 feet high and 25 feet in diameter at the base. Thirty cords of pinion pine and juniper were put into each oven and a fire was started. The fire's intensity was controlled by adjusting small doors in the oven. After about twelve days of burning, the fire was smothered by closing the vents. Each oven made 300 bushels of charcoal—enough to barbecue seven million hamburgers.

Finding the site: To reach the Ward Charcoal Ovens, drive south from Ely on US 50/6/93 for 7 miles, reaching the well-marked turnoff to the ovens. This is Cave Valley Road. Follow it southeast for 11 miles to the site.

For more information: Ward Charcoal Ovens State Historic Park, P.O. Box 151761, Ely, NV 89315; (775) 867-3001 (Northern Region Office) or (775) 289-1693 (Ranger Station); http://parks.nv.gov/ww.htm

Museums

Museums, especially some of the smaller ones, are not only good places to get in touch with the history of an area, but are often sources for local rockhounding information. Following are a few of Nevada's museums. Don't take this list as definitive, though; also look in local phone books and keep your eyes open as you drive through the small towns.

Boulder City-Hoover Dam Museum
1305 Arizona St.
Boulder City, NV 89005
(702) 294-1988

Northeastern Nevada Museum
1515 Idaho St.
Elko, NV 89801
(775) 738-3418

Central Nevada Museum
1900 Logan Field Rd.
Tonopah, NV 89049
(775) 482-9676

Nevada Northern Railway Museum
1100 Ave. A
East Ely, NV 89301
(775) 289-2085

Liberty Engine Company
117 South C St.
Virginia City, NV 89440
(775) 847-0717

White Pine Public Museum, Inc.
2000 Aultman St.
Ely, NV 89301
(775) 289-4710

Mark Twain's Museum of Memories
4753 South C St.
Virginia City, NV 89440
(775) 847-0525

Lost City Museum
721 S. Moapa Valley Blvd.
Overton, NV 89040
(702) 397-2193

Humboldt County Museum
175 Museum Ave.
Winnemucca, NV 89446
(775) 623-2912

Sixteen Trips for the Intrepid Explorer

If you buy a lottery ticket every week in the hope that you will strike it rich, or if you buy those little grab bags at rock and gem shows, you will love these sites. Some are sites that I have heard about, but have not had a chance to visit. Some are sites I have visited, but did not find enough to warrant sending you there with a promise of success. Some I have visited and found nothing, but have that feeling there must be something there. I don't think you will find any supermarkets or malls at any of these sites, since most are in remote areas, but you might come away with nothing more exciting than sunburn, mosquito bites, and sore feet.

I offer these sites with no guarantees. On the other hand, you just might make a great find. A few years ago I received a letter from a lady in Italy who, while visiting the United States, bought a copy of *Rockhounding Utah,* followed directions to a remote site near the Salt Flats, and picked up an eleven-ounce silver nugget. Is your appetite whetted?

Hubbard Basin
About the site: This is an old collecting area where I feel sure you will find some nice petrified wood. The pieces will probably be small, since some years

ago the BLM opened the area to commercial collecting. Cora and I got within a mile or so of the site in the fall of 1996, and from the condition of the road, it looked like every dump truck in North America had been in and out of there. We had some conflicting information and didn't go far enough to reach the site. If you go, I strongly recommend a four-wheel-drive vehicle. The ruts in many places were 2- and 3-feet deep.

Finding the site: From Jackpot, drive south on US 93 for about 30 miles to a road marked for O'Neill (on the right). Take this road for about 3.9 miles to a dirt track heading right. This is where the going gets rough. Follow the rough dirt track for about 8 miles. At this point, you should be in the middle of the collecting area. With all of the commercial activity that has taken place here, it should be easy to spot.

Palisade

About the site: Agate and jasper have been reported at Palisade for a long time. When I got there, I found two sets of railroad tracks instead of the one that my directions had. To make matters worse, the tracks were separated by the Humboldt River, which had about a 6-foot drop-off at each bank. I paralleled the tracks and river for a couple of miles, but could see no way to get to the east side, where an old mine was supposed to have agate on the tailings. We ran out of time (and I ran out of patience), so we went on to bigger and better sites. I still think that a little local inquiry and a little walking would bear some fruit. If you are in the area, it is easy to get to Palisade, and it is just 0.5 mile or so off the highway.

Finding the site: From Elko, drive west on I-70 for 22 miles to Carlin. Turn south at Carlin on NV Star Route 278. At 10 miles you will see a sign to Palisade. The town is about 0.5 mile west of the highway.

Jack Creek

About the site: When Cora and I were at Copper Basin, we stayed so long looking through the shale at the fossils that time ran out. I made a valiant effort to get to Jarbidge, but it was getting too late, so we turned back. I understand that the road to Jarbidge and Jack Creek is about like the one to Copper Basin. This was a good dirt road, but a little washboardy in spots. The main disadvantage is the distance. There are about 40-plus miles of dirt each way, and it seems like an eternity getting there. If you have the time, you should probably give it a try. You may find some nice agate, and the town of Jarbidge is said to be a really interesting spot (see Sights along the Way).

Finding the site: From Copper Basin, go north about 10 miles to Jarbidge. From Jarbidge, continue north for about 3.5 miles. At this point the road crosses Jack Creek. Go east into Jack Canyon to a fork. There is supposed to be seam agate here.

Tuscarora Area

About the site: The area west and south of Tuscarora is covered with old mines. In addition to gold and silver, a lot of top-quality turquoise was taken out of here. It would be foolish to try to pinpoint locations, since the area is so vast. The old town of Midas would be a good place to center a search. The Rand mine near there has given up good samples of cinnabar in opal. About 40 miles or so southwest of Tuscarora is the Silver Cloud mine, where more cinnabar in opalite has been reported. There have also been reports of agate, chalcedony, and petrified wood in the area. If you have a camper or motor home with a four-wheel-drive vehicle hanging on behind, you are set for a trip to this area. Set up a camp and roam to your heart's content.

Finding the site: From Tuscarora drive west toward Midas. There are lots of roads to explore, so just pick one and start searching. If you need a little more structure to your search, you might want to inquire in Tuscarora. There is a post office there that might provide some help.

Paradise Valley

About the site: There is a lot of rockhounding to be done north of Winnemucca, and some of the best is reported to be in the area around the town of Paradise Valley. I don't know if they had rockhounds in mind when they named it Paradise, but from the reports I've heard, they certainly could have. The area around Hinckey Summit is reported to have lots of opal, agate, cinnabar, jasper, petrified wood, and an occasional geode.

Finding the site: From Winnemucca, go north on US 95 for about 22 miles to the junction with NV 290. At about 12 to 14 miles, Sheldon Road goes right. Follow this toward Chimney Dam Reservoir. It is in this general area that the petrified wood has been found.

To find other treasures, backtrack to NV 290, and continue on to Paradise Valley. From there, head north about 10 to 12 miles to Hinckey Summit. Search along the road on both sides of the summit for opal, agate, and cinnabar. I have no specific sites, so you will have to do some driving, walking, and searching. As usual, a little local inquiry will probably help a lot. You might also try the chamber of commerce in Winnemucca before you start. Years ago they put out a little rockhounding book. Although it is no longer available, I'll bet they can put you in touch with someone who can pinpoint some areas for you.

Leonard Creek

About the site: This is another site that I have not yet visited. It covers a vast area, and good hunting is reported almost everywhere. The material reported here is opal (some dendritic and some fluorescent), agate, obsidian, petrified wood, sphalerite, and rhyolite. Much of the area is very remote, so be sure to take the proper precautions before venturing out. It would be a good idea to check with the chamber of commerce in Winnemucca for more specific information on these sites before you begin your trip.

Finding the site: *Site A:* From the junction of US 95 and NV 140 north of Winnemucca, drive west on NV 140 for about 36 miles to Leonard Creek Road. Follow this road for about 4 miles to a point where it turns southwest. Continue on for about 5 more miles to a fork. Hunt around both sides of the left fork for 1 mile or so.

Site B: From the junction of US 95 and NV 140 north of Winnemucca, drive north on US 95 to the junction with NV 293 at Orovada. Drive west on NV 293 for about 8 miles. At this point, the Riverside Ranch Road goes left, back to NV 140. Hunt around all sides of the fork.

Site C: From the fork at Site B, continue north on NV 293 toward Sentinel Rock. Try any side roads in the Sentinel Rock area.

Nightingale

About the site: This is another site about which I have very little information. It is quite a way out into the boondocks, but it just might be rewarding. Calcite, garnet, and scheelite have been reported on the tailings at old mines in the Nightingale mining district.

Finding the site: From Lovelock, drive south on I-80 to exit 93. The road here may be marked Ragged Top Road or Nightingale Road. Follow the road west for about 14 miles to a fork. Take the left fork for about 18 miles to another fork. Take the right-hand fork for another 10 miles or so. At this point you should see a number of mines to explore.

Star Peak

About the site: I have only sketchy information about this site, but the prospect of finding agate geodes always gets my attention. In addition, it looks like a pretty easy site to get to, so I've included it just in case you want to try, too.

Finding the site: From Mill City, on I-80 north of Lovelock, drive south on NV 400 for 10 to 12 miles. Star Peak is to the right and about 5 miles away. Look for roads going that way and head for the peak. The collecting is said to be on the eastern slope.

Getchell Mine

About the site: I included this because I have not been there and I am itching to go. This is a famous mine, not so much for the gold it produced, but for the beautiful mineral specimens that have been found there. Among the minerals on this list are cinnabar, fluorite, galkhaite, getchellite, gypsum, molybdenite, scheelite, orpiment, and realgar. The realgar sometimes occurs as deep red crystals in a translucent white calcite. If the photos I've seen are even close, this is truly spectacular stuff. I'm sure they are not just lying around on the dumps, but one can always hope. My information is old, so remember to check and see if the mine is working or is posted.

Finding the site: It would be a good idea to inquire in Winnemucca for directions to the Getchell. I can give reasonable directions, but since I have not been there and have not found any specific directions, I might send you to British Columbia. (Of course that's nice, too.) A short distance east of the little town of Golconda, a road goes left toward Midas. It is probably marked, but I'm not sure. About 16 miles out on this road, you will come to a fork. The right fork goes on to Midas, and the left goes north to the Getchell Mine. From the fork, it looks like about another 20 to 25 miles to the mine. Remember, these mileages are best guesses from a number of maps. If you get there and find something, write and tell me about it.

Majuba Mine

About the site: This site, like the Getchell Mine, has been a collector's dream for years, and another one I have not been to, but am anxious to visit. It has produced specimens of anatase, arsenopyrite, bornite, brookite, cassiterite, chalcopyrite, enargite, molybdenite, pyrrhotite, pyrite, arthurite, azurite, brochanite, chalcanthite, chalcocite, chrysocolla, copper, cuprite, gypsum, limonite, olivenite, fluorite, orthoclase, quartz, and zeunerite. Better take a big rock bag. If you do decide to take this trip, be sure to check locally on the collecting status. My information is old, and this mine has been closed to collectors from time to time in the past.

Finding the site: It would be a good idea to check locally for specific directions before you start. But, although I have not been to the mine, it looks like a pretty easy spot to find. From Imlay, take the road around the north end of Rye Patch Reservoir and head out to the west. In about 12 miles a road will go southwest. Follow this for about 4 or 5 miles to Majuba Mountain and the Majuba Mine.

Gabbs Area

About the site: This is supposed to be a site for opalized wood, but Cora and I spent an hour or so here and found only some little pieces of opalite. The main collecting area is supposed to be around the gray hills. The ground is soft, so if you are given to digging, you might well find some nice material. There is a lot of area out here to search, so give yourself more time than we did, and you may be well rewarded.

Finding the site: From the intersection of NV 361 and NV 844 about 1.5 miles north of Gabbs, drive north on NV 361 for about 1.5 miles to a road going left. Follow this road for about 10 miles to another road going right. Take this road for 2 miles. At this point, you will see the gray hills on your right. Hunt all over the area.

Bell Canyon

About the site: I visited this area in the fall of 1996, but didn't find enough to make it a site in the book. I did find quite a bit of bubbly chalcedony on the top of the hills to the right of the road. In itself it wasn't much to look at, but much of it fluoresces a pretty green under ultraviolet light. If you are looking for something that will fluoresce, you can find it here, and you might also find some of the jasper and geodes that have been reported here.

Finding the site: From the intersection of US 50 and NV 839, 36 miles east of Fallon, drive south on NV 839 for 7 miles to a road going left. Follow this road for about 3 miles. From this point, hunt along the hilltops on the right side of the road for the next 3 miles or so.

Quartz Mountain

About the site: This site is just across the highway from the turnoff to Sites 61 and 62. It is easy to get to. The road is good and there are tons of tailings to hunt on. The problem is that I hunted and found very little. The tailings are all over—up the hill behind the mine, too, and I didn't climb up there to look. I just have this feeling that there might be some nice mineral specimens at this site. You might take the ultraviolet lamp along. There is always a possibility that some nice fluorescent minerals are lurking in the tailings.

Finding the site: From the turnoff on NV 361 to Sites 61 and 62, go north on NV 361 for about 0.2 mile to a road marked for Broken Hills, going east. Follow this road past the old Broken Hills mine for about 3 miles to a fork. Go right at the fork for about 1.2 miles. At this point, you will see the Quartz Mountain mine on the right. Take the dirt road over to the tailings and begin your hunt.

Little Antelope Summit

About the site: This is a spot that I visited in the fall of 1996 and found only chips of the reported wonderstone. The site is only a few tenths of a mile from the highway, and it stands to reason that it would be pretty well picked over. However, the chips I found were spectacular. I know I said I would not editorialize, but I just can't help it. The big brothers and sisters of these chips would really be something. The material looked more like opalite than the usual rhyolite wonderstone and was certainly worth another trip. There is a lot of country beyond the road, and if you have the time (which I didn't) roam around and see what you can find.

Finding the site: From Ely, drive northwest on US 50 for about 40 miles to Little Antelope Summit. At the summit, you will see a turnout to the right. Drive in as far as you can and begin your hunt.

New York Canyon

About the site: This site was featured in the first edition. It has been famous for fossils such as ammonites for years, and the upper reaches of the canyon contain many old mines with numerous minerals and lots of malachite and azurite specimens. Unfortunately, the road has deteriorated to the point where spots are just boulder crawling. I decided that most readers would not like to beat up their vehicles, so I decided not to feature this site in the second edition. If you are a rock crawler, you may well be rewarded with some nice material and/or fossils. Of course, the thrill of the find might be tempered by the repair bill on your vehicle.

Finding the site: If you are ready to tackle the trip, start at the junction of US 95 and NV 361 just north of Luning and drive southeast on US 95 for 0.7 mile to the rest stop. Turn left into the rest stop and right at the dirt road. Follow the road as it parallels US 95 and the alkali lake on the left. At 0.7 mile from the rest stop, a road goes left across the dry lake. Follow this road. After you cross the lake, you will come to a fork. Take the right fork and follow it for just over 5 miles as it winds up into the canyon. Park wherever you find a wide spot and hunt for fossils in the cliffs.

Valley of Fire

About the site: Because of a very rough road, the two Valley of Fire sites in the first edition were left out of this second edition and replaced with two that are much easier to get to. If you are intrepid, though, give the two excluded sites a try. I suspect that you will be rewarded with some nice cutting material. The two sites have been hunted for a long, long time, but there is still stuff there.

Finding the site: To get to the sites, follow the Valley of Fire directions in this guide (page 226), but continue on toward Buffington Pockets. At 5.1 miles from the BUFFINGTON POCKETS sign, you will be at the top of a hill. Turn right on the track and drive about 0.4 mile to the base of the cliff on the left. Park on the flat and hunt all over the area. To reach the second site, return to the road, turn right, and drive 0.5 mile. There are several tracks heading over to the cliff on the left. The cliff has lots of agate seams. Good luck.

Map Legend

═══{101}═══	U.S. Highway
═══(1)═══	State Highway
═══════	Local/Gravel Road
=======:	Unimproved Road
------------	4-Wheel Drive Road
⊢+⊢+⊢+⊢	Railroad Tracks
～～～	River/Creek
--·--·--	Intermittent Stream
�⟩	Spring
⎯·⎯·⎯	National Forest/Park
⬭	Pit Mine
⬭	Alkali Flat
⏜	Bridge
▲	Camping
▭	Cattle Guard
⫶	Gate
▲	Mountain Peak
NO!	No Collecting/No Access/Wrong Way
🅿	Parking
■	Point of Interest/Structure
⚒	Rockhounding Site
75	Site Locator
○	Town
❀	Viewpoint/Overlook

Cold Springs Valley Road: Chrysocolla, Malachite

Land type: Hills
Elevation: 5,010 feet
GPS: N39 38.93' / W119 57.45'
Best season: Spring through fall
Land manager: BLM
Material: Malachite, chrysocolla
Tools: Rock hammer
Vehicle: Any
Special attractions: Lake Tahoe area
Accommodations: Motels, RV parking in Reno area
Finding the site: From the intersection of US 395 and I-80 in Reno, drive northwest on US 395 for 12.6 miles to the Cold Springs Valley turnoff (exit 80). Go right on the blacktop and immediately turn right again into the small dirt parking area at the foot of the hill. You will see the tailings all the way to the top of the hill.

The chrysocolla pieces at Cold Springs Valley Road are small, but a very nice, deep blue.

Rockhounding

There is a lot of material to be found here, and it is easy to spot. Most is malachite or chrysocolla, but azurite, hematite, and many other mineral specimens have also been reported here. I found all of my specimens on the lower tailings piles, but better material has been reported on the tailings at the top of the hill. Put on your hiking boots and give it a try.

NOTE: Watch out for snakes at this site. I was given fair warning by a medium-size rattler about halfway up the hill. Don't bypass this great site because of it, but do be aware and take the usual precautions.

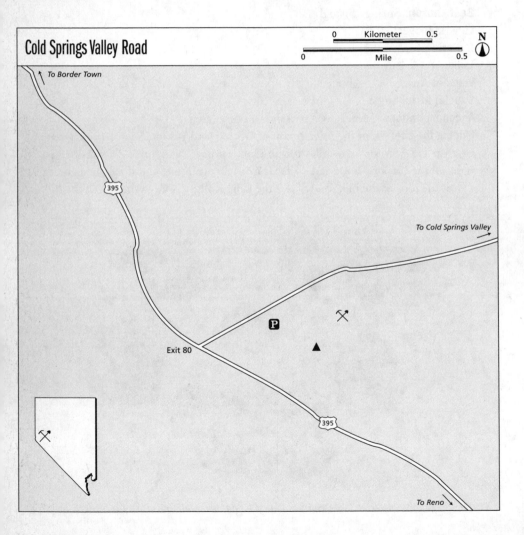

Pipeline Road: Agate

Land type: Hills
Elevation: 4,350 feet
GPS: N39 32.08' / W119 14.20'
Best season: Spring through fall
Land manager: BLM
Material: Agate
Tools: Rock hammer
Vehicle: High clearance
Special attractions: None
Accommodations: Motels in Fernley; open camping on BLM land
Finding the site: From the intersection of US 50A and US 95A in Fernley, drive 4.7 miles south on US 95A. At this point, there is a sign pointing to a speedway and a dirt road heading right. Turn onto this road and turn immediately onto a rough dirt track that loops back to the north and parallels the highway. Follow this track for about 0.5 mile to a fence and a track going left. Take the track to the left along the fence for 0.4 mile. Park anywhere and hunt in all directions from the fence.

NOTE: The track from the highway to the site was pretty rough on my last visit. It is alright for high-clearance vehicles, but four-wheel drive would be a plus. If your vehicle can't make it, see the note for an alternate route for the Hilltop site (Site 3).

Rockhounding

The agate in this area is scattered and generally small, but a little patience and a lot of walking will allow you to collect some nice pieces large enough for 30 x 40 mm cabs.

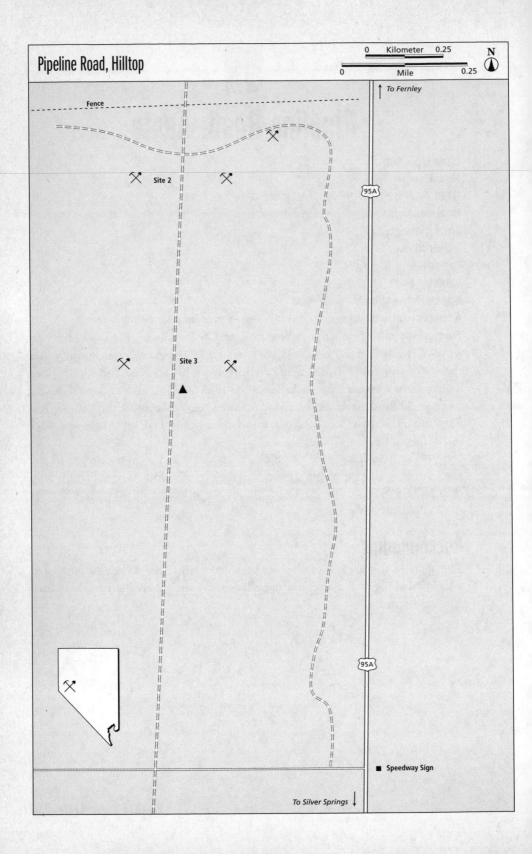

Pipeline Road, Hilltop

0   Kilometer   0.25

0   Mile   0.25

N

To Fernley

Fence

Site 2

95A

Site 3

95A

Speedway Sign

To Silver Springs

Hilltop: Agate

See map on page 38.
Land type: Hills
Elevation: 4,600 feet
GPS: N39 31.66' / W119 13.96'
Best season: Spring through fall
Land manager: BLM
Material: Agate
Tools: Rock hammer
Vehicle: High clearance
Special attractions: None
Accommodations: Motels in Fernley; open camping on BLM land
Finding the site: From the intersection of US 50A and US 95A in Fernley, drive 4.7 miles south on US 95A. At this point, there is a sign pointing to a speedway and a dirt road heading right. Turn onto this road and drive for 0.2 mile to an intersection with another dirt road. Take this road to the right and proceed to the foot of the high hill. Drive up if you can, or hike if you must.

View looking down the hill at Site 3. Agate is scattered on both sides of the road on the hilltop.

There is scattered agate all along the hill, but the best material is at the top, so if you have four-wheel drive or a high clearance pickup, you can drive up and park. If your vehicle can't make it, just hike the short distance.

Rockhounding

If you hike far enough on the flat where you park, you will find some nice pieces of agate, but the best seems to be at the top of the

Agate from the Hilltop site. Colors are predominantly yellow, blue, and white.

hill. Hike up the hill and keep a sharp eye out all the way. This is not the most prolific agate field in Nevada, but if you take some time and do some walking, you will come away with some good pieces.

Gas Line Road: Agate

Land type: Low hills
Elevation: 4,700 feet
GPS: N 39 30.48' / W119 13.43' (GPS data taken at the highway gate)
Best season: Spring through fall
Land manager: BLM
Material: Agate
Tools: Rock hammer
Vehicle: Any
Special attractions: None
Accommodations: Motels in Fernley; open camping on BLM land

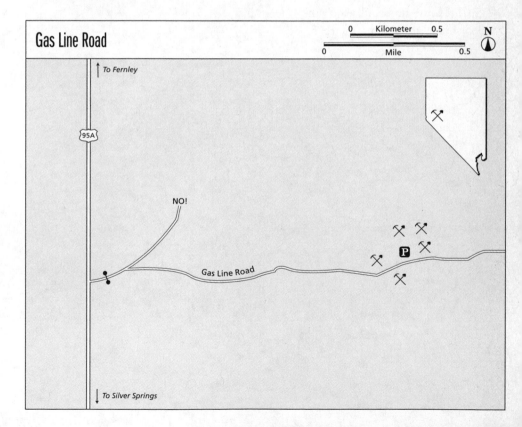

Finding the site: From the intersection of US 50A and US 95A in Fernley, drive south on US 95A for 7.1 miles to a road going east. Go through the gate and follow the road for 1.7 miles from the highway. At this point, there is a wide area for parking.

Rockhounding

The agate is scattered for quite a distance on both sides of the road. It is typical of the agate found in the area—rather small, but with occasional pieces showing nice color and/or patterns. Spend some time and search the low hills farther along the road.

The agate is small but colorful at the Gas Line Road site. This sample is yellow, tan, and orange with hints of blue.

Chalcedony Hill: Chalcedony

Land type: Hill and road cut
Elevation: 4,500 feet
GPS: N39 26.88' / W119 13.51'
Best season: Any
Land manager: BLM; Nevada Department of Transportation
Material: Chalcedony
Tools: Rock hammer, chisels
Vehicle: Any
Special attractions: None
Accommodations: Motels in Fernley; beach camping at Lake Lahontan State Recreation Area; open camping on BLM land
Finding the site: From the intersection of US 50 and US 95 in Silver Springs, drive north on US 95A for 2.2 miles to a large road cut and hill on the left.

This is Chalcedony Hill. Nice bubbly pieces of fluorescent chalcedony can be found all over the hill.

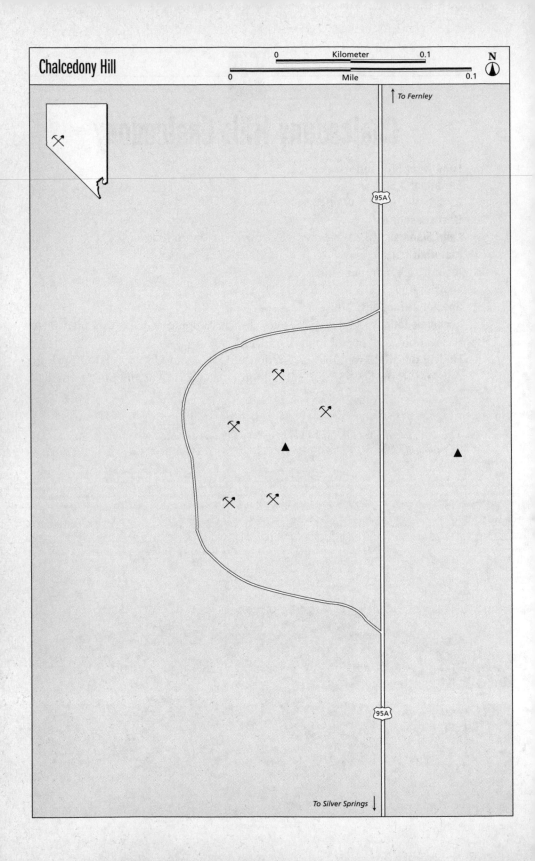

Chalcedony Hill

0   Kilometer   0.1

0   Mile   0.1

N

To Fernley

95A

95A

To Silver Springs

There is a road that runs around the hill and returns to the highway. Park anywhere along the side or back of the hill.

Rockhounding

This is an interesting site for some nice little pieces of bubbly and banded chalcedony. There are lots of pieces on the hill, and more in seams in the rocks on the hill. Try searching the face of the cut on the smaller hill on the east side of the road, too. A plus is that much of the material fluoresces green under shortwave ultraviolet light.

Pretty sample of fluorescent chalcedony from Chalcedony Hill.

Lahontan Reservoir: Agate

Land type: Flat along railroad tracks
Elevation: 4,200 feet
GPS: N39 27.14' / W119 05.16'
Best season: Any
Land manager: BLM
Material: Agate
Tools: Rock hammer
Vehicle: Any
Special attractions: Lahontan State Recreation Area
Accommodations: Motels in Fernley; open camping on BLM lands; beach camping at Lahontan State Recreation Area

I don't know how this piece of caramel brown agate knew that it would be found at Site 6, but rocks are funny that way.

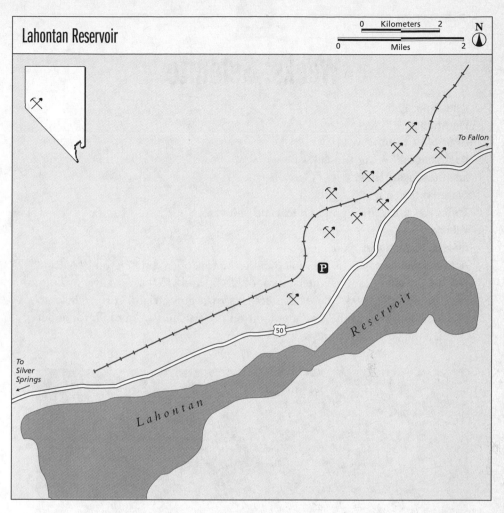

0 Kilometers 2

0 Miles 2

N

To Fallon

To
Silver
Springs

50

Reservoir

Lahontan

Finding the site: From Silver Springs, drive east on US 50. At about 8 miles, you will begin to see the lake on the right and the railroad tracks near the road on the left. Find a place to park off the highway next to the tracks.

Rockhounding

This is not a terribly productive site, but some nice small pieces of agate may be found by walking along the tracks and looking at the berms that heavy equipment has turned up. The big plus is the recreation area across the highway. If you are camping or boating, why not cross the road and do a little close-by rockhounding? You may find a real jewel, and you won't have to drive down 80 miles of bad road to do it.

SITE 7

Weeks: Selenite

Land type: Hills
Elevation: 4,500 feet
GPS: N39 15.69' / W119 17.76'
Best season: Spring and fall
Land manager: BLM
Material: Selenite
Tools: Rock hammer, putty knife, hand cultivator
Vehicle: Any
Special attractions: None
Accommodations: Motels in Fernley and Yerington; open camping on BLM land
Finding the site: From the intersection of US 50 and US 95A in Silver Springs, drive south on US 95A for 11.2 miles to a road going right. Turn right onto this road, go through the gate, and hunt on the flats in the low hills for about 2 miles and at the old mine.

Cora searches the hillside for selenite at the Weeks site.

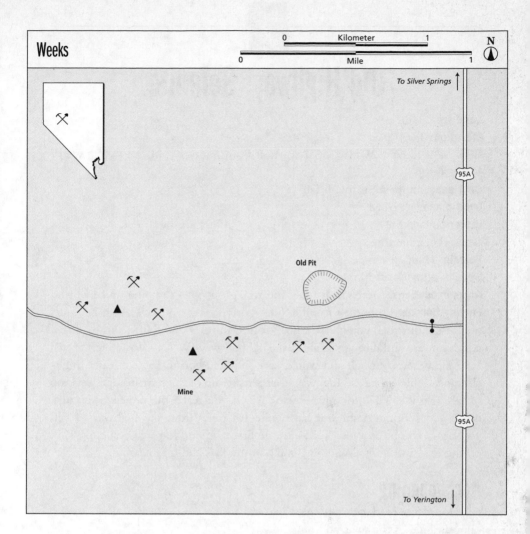

0   Kilometer   1

0   Mile   1

N

To Silver Springs

95A

Old Pit

95A

Mine

To Yerington

Rockhounding

This is a really nice site for some fine, clear selenite crystals. You simply can't miss it if it's a sunny day. The ground and the hills sparkle with selenite. Your biggest problem will be in deciding which specimens to take and which to leave for me.

Three good selenite samples from Weeks.

Old Highway: Selenite

Land type: Hills
Elevation: 4,600 feet
GPS: N39 13.67' / W119 13.70' (turnoff from highway); N39 14.90' / W119 13.98' (site)
Best season: Spring through fall
Land manager: BLM
Material: Selenite
Tools: Rock hammer
Vehicle: High clearance
Special attractions: None
Accommodations: Motels in Fernley and Yerington; open camping on BLM land
Finding the site: From the turnoff to Site 7, drive south on US 95A for 2.7 miles to a rough dirt road going east. Check your odometer and follow this road as it winds upward and through a gate to the old highway. (When I was there, the first 0.3 mile was very rough and would have required you to have at least a high-clearance vehicle. The old highway itself is made up of the remains of a blacktop surface and is suitable for any vehicle.) When you reach the old highway, turn north and continue until you have gone 1.5 miles from the highway. At this point, you will be at a long road cut (the first road cut you will come to). Park off the road and hunt along the cut and in the flats and hills nearby.

Rockhounding

All along the road cut, on the opposite side of the road, and on the flats, you can find some nice selenite crystals. They are not as clear or as plentiful as those at Weeks (Site 7), but they are worth collecting. I don't know how far the old pavement goes, but there are some interesting white cuts in the distance. If you have some time, you might want to do a little exploring.

A nice selenite sample from the Old Highway site near Weeks.

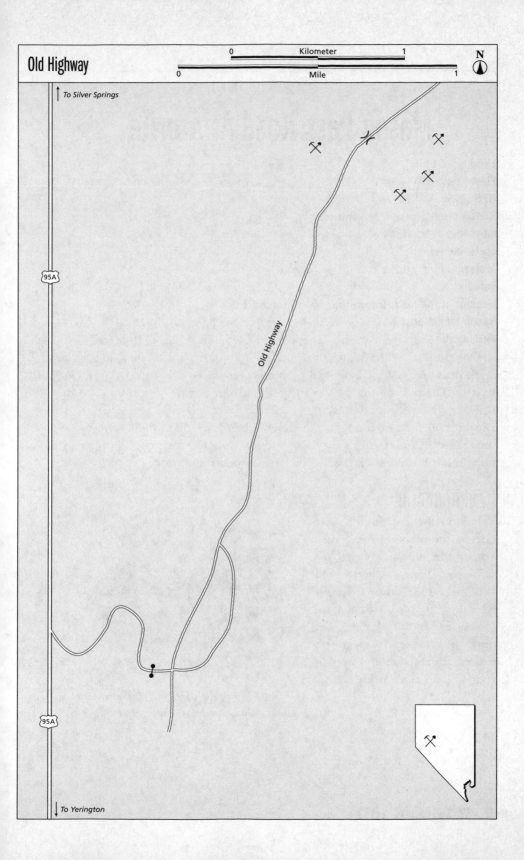

Old Highway

N

0   Kilometer   1

0   Mile   1

To Silver Springs

95A

Old Highway

95A

To Yerington

Mason Pass Road A: Azurite

Land type: Hills
Elevation: 5,000 feet
GPS: N39 02.12' / W119 15.26'
Best season: Spring through fall
Land manager: BLM
Material: Azurite
Tools: Rock hammer
Vehicle: Any
Special attractions: Interesting old mining area
Accommodations: Motels in Yerington; open camping on BLM land
Finding the site: At the west side of Yerington, US 95A makes a 90-degree turn to the north. Take US 95A north for 2.2 miles to Luzier Lane. The road is well marked and there is an additional sign directing you to the Walker River. Go west on Luzier Lane for 2 miles to the intersection with Mason Pass Road. Drive north on Mason Pass Road. At 2.2 miles, you will come to a stop sign at a main truck road from one of the mines. When I was there, there were some very big trucks using this road, so be careful. Continue on past the stop sign for another 1.5 miles on Mason Pass Road, pull off, and park.

Rockhounding

Search in the cut on the west side of the road for some nice azurite specimens. They are just stains, but they are pretty and will make nice displays. If you have the time, try hunting above the cut and to the west. A lot of turquoise has been found in this general area. I didn't find any, but you just might get lucky.

Light colors in the photo are blue azurite stains. This material is abundant at Site 9 on Mason Pass Road.

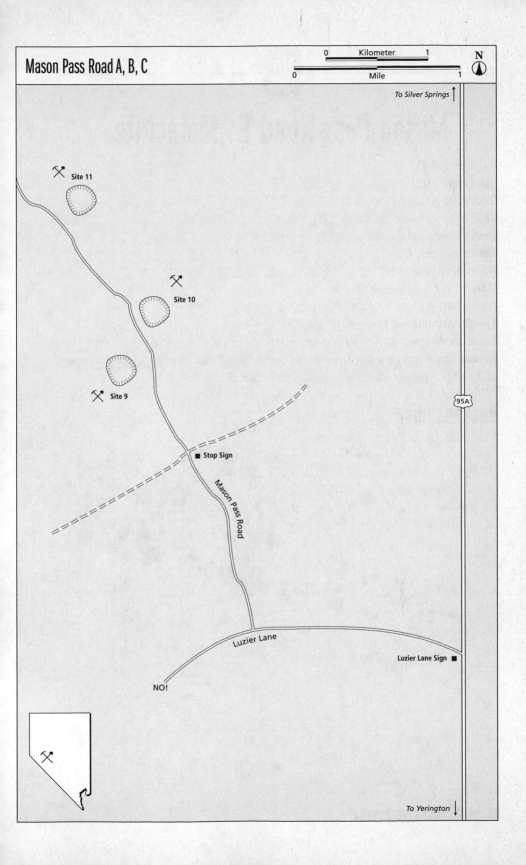

Mason Pass Road A, B, C

0 Kilometer 1
0 Mile 1

N

To Silver Springs

Site 11

Site 10

Site 9

95A

Stop Sign

Mason Pass Road

Luzier Lane

Luzier Lane Sign

NO!

To Yerington

Mason Pass Road B: Malachite

See map on page 53.

Land type: Hills
Elevation: 5,100 feet
GPS: N39 01.80' / W119 15.51'
Best season: Spring through fall
Land manager: BLM
Material: Malachite
Tools: Rock hammer
Vehicle: Any
Special attractions: Interesting old mining area
Accommodations: Motels in Yerington; open camping on BLM land
Finding the site: From Site 9, continue north on Mason Pass Road for 0.4 mile to an old mine site and some tailings on the right. Park off the road.

Rockhounding

There are some nice pieces of malachite on and around the tailings. Like the azurite at Site 9, they are stained and not suitable for lapidary work, but the colorful chunks make nice displays.

Malachite stains on white quartz from Mason Pass Road.

Mason Pass Road C: Epidote in Granite

See map on page 53.
Land type: Hills
Elevation: 5,200 feet
GPS: N39 00.93' / W119 16.01'
Best season: Spring through fall
Land manager: BLM
Material: White granite with green epidote
Tools: Rock hammer
Vehicle: Any
Special attractions: Interesting old mining area
Accommodations: Motels in Yerington; open camping on BLM lands
Finding the site: From Site 10, continue north on Mason Pass Road for another 1.1 miles, pull off the road, and park.

Rockhounding

Hunt in the washes and flats along the east side of the road for nice pieces of white granite with green epidote crystals. This is interesting material for display, but also makes nice pen stands, desk accessories, or other miscellaneous things. It takes a good polish and could be used for cabochons as well. Where is it written that you can't have granite jewelry?

Green epidote in granite from Mason Pass Road C, Site 11.

Trinity Mountains A: Opal

Land type: Mountains
Elevation: 5,900 feet
GPS: N40 10.30' / W118 43.30'
Best season: Spring through fall
Land manager: BLM
Material: Common opal
Tools: Rock hammer, chisels
Vehicle: High clearance
Special attractions: None
Accommodations: Motels in Lovelock; RV parking and camping at Rye Patch State Recreation Area; open camping on BLM land
Finding the site: From the middle of Lovelock, take Main Street west for a couple of blocks to where it makes a tricky turn south and back to the west. At this point, you will be on Western Avenue. Continue west on Western Avenue for 3.1 miles to a fork. The right fork goes to the dump. (Who knows, maybe

The microwave tower at Trinity Mountains A, Site 12. Opal is found on the flanks of the hill to the right of the tower.

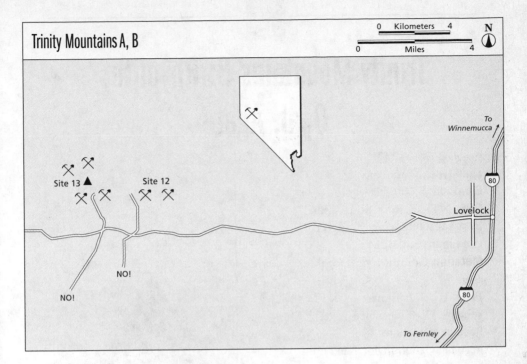

0 Kilometers 4

0 Miles 4

N

To Winnemucca

80

Lovelock

Site 13 ▲

Site 12

NO!

NO!

To Fernley

someone dumped some rocks?) It is probably better to take the left fork and continue west. At 10 miles, a road goes right. Keep straight ahead. At 0.2 mile beyond this road, you will come to a fork. Keep to the right. At 1.2 miles from this fork, a road goes right into the hills. Take this road for 1.2 miles to a microwave tower. There is a wide area just above the tower where you can park.

Rockhounding

Hunt all around the tower and on the slopes to the east. There is common opal in a variety of colors ranging from white to brown. I almost called the brown "root beer," but that would violate my ban on descriptive adjectives. Whatever beauty you ascribe to the opal, there is a lot of it here. The slopes are a little steep, so keep an eye on the kids.

White opal in black matrix from Trinity Mountains A, Site 12.

Trinity Mountains B: Rhyolite, Opal, Agate

See map on page 57.
Land type: Mountains
Elevation: 5,600 feet
GPS: N40 10.18' / W118 43.98'
Best season: Spring through fall
Land manager: BLM
Material: Common opal, opalite, agate
Tools: Rock hammer
Vehicle: High clearance
Special attractions: None
Accommodations: Motels in Lovelock; RV parking and camping at Rye Patch State Recreation Area; open camping on BLM lands
Finding the site: From the turnoff to the microwave tower at Site 12, continue on west on the main road for 0.3 mile to a fork. Keep right at the fork and drive another 0.3 mile to a multiple fork. Take the far right fork for 1.1 miles to the eroded pillar to the north. Park anywhere and hunt all around the area.

Botryoidal structures on opalite from the peak at Site 13.

Rockhounding

This is an old collecting area that looks as though it has been visited by every rockhound in the western hemisphere. There is still a lot here, though, so be sure to do a thorough search. Visit all sides of the pillar and range outward as far as you have time and energy to do. You've come a long way and you don't want to go home empty-handed (and you won't).

A view of the peak at Site 13. Material is found all around the base and on the flanks of the tower.

...le Picher Mine Area A: Opalized Wood, Agate, Opalite

Land type: Hills
Elevation: 5,400 feet
GPS: N40 16.54' / W118 45.02'
Best season: Spring through fall
Land manager: BLM
Material: Agate, opalite, opalized wood
Tools: Rock hammer
Vehicle: Any
Special attractions: None
Accommodations: Motels in Lovelock; RV parking and camping at Rye Patch State Recreation Area; open camping on BLM land

Nice pieces of opalized wood are found at the foot of the hill at Site 14, on the way to the Eagle Picher Mine.

Eagle Picher Mine Areas A, B, C, D

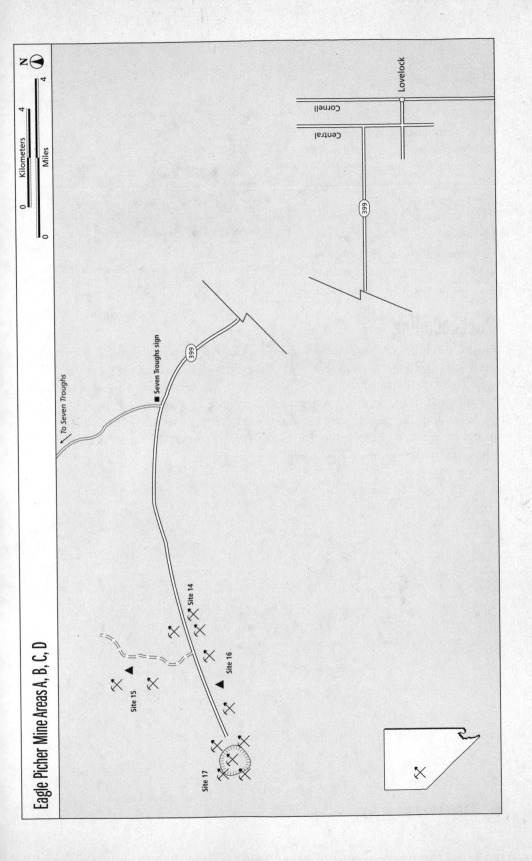

Finding the site: From the center of Lovelock, go west on 14th Street for 0.2 mile to Central Avenue. Turn north (right) on Central Avenue and go 1.2 miles. At this point, turn left on NV 399. (This road is known locally as the Seven Troughs Road.) Drive 12.2 miles. Keep left on the blacktop at the Seven Troughs sign and continue on NV 399 another 6.3 miles to a parking area on the right.

Banded opalite from the Eagle Picher mine at Site 14. Colors are tan and white.

Rockhounding

At the parking area, you will see where rockhounds have high-graded their finds. This will give you a general idea of the type of material available in the area. There is a lot to be found here, but the best will take some roaming over the hills and in the washes. I found some very nice opalized wood about 50 yards north of the parking area, but you should definitely search on both sides of the road. Much of the opalite and opalized wood found here will fluoresce green under shortwave ultraviolet light.

Eagle Picher Mine Area B: Opalite

See map on page 61.
Land type: Hills
Elevation: 5,124 feet
GPS: N40 16.14' / W118 46.12'
Best season: Spring through fall
Land manager: BLM
Material: Opalite
Tools: Rock hammer
Vehicle: Any
Special attractions: None
Accommodations: Motels in Lovelock; RV parking and camping at Rye Patch State Recreation Area; open camping on BLM land
Finding the site: From Site 14, drive 1.2 miles to a road on the right. Follow this road as it winds along some low hills. Park anywhere near the hills and hunt all over them.

Rockhounding

These hills contain a lot of opalite. Because the heat and the weather are hard on the surface material, it is best to do a little easy digging in the sandy soil for the better material.

Eagle Picher Mine Area C: Opalite

See map on page 61.

Land type: Hills
Elevation: 5,000 feet
GPS: N40 16.18' / W118 46.64'
Best season: Spring through fall
Land manager: BLM
Material: Opalite
Tools: Rock hammer
Vehicle: Any
Special attractions: None
Accommodations: Motels in Lovelock; RV parking and camping at Rye Patch State Recreation Area; open camping on BLM land
Finding the site: From the turnoff to Site 15, continue west on the blacktop road for 0.3 mile. Park off the road and hunt on and around the white hill on the south side of the road.

Rockhounding

There is opalite all over the top of the white hill, and you will find more in the little wash on the east side of the hill. Opalite is easy to find here, but you can find it almost everywhere along this road if you are persistent. Take only the best, because when you see what's at Site 17, you might just throw away most of what you found here.

Eagle Picher Mine Area D: Opalite

See map on page 61.

Land type: Old, open pit mine

Elevation: 4,900 feet

GPS: N40 16.16' / W118 47.34'

Best season: Spring through fall

Land manager: Unknown

Material: Opalite

Tools: Rock hammer

Vehicle: Any

Special attractions: None

Accommodations: Motels in Lovelock; RV parking and camping at Rye Patch State Recreation Area; open camping on BLM land

Finding the site: From Site 16, continue on NV 399 for 0.8 mile to the end of the pavement. Park anywhere and search in the old pit.

The huge pit in the Eagle Picher mine area still holds a lot of nice opalite.

Rockhounding

This is one of those areas where I couldn't find just who the land manager is. The pit is old, it has no posting of any kind, there is no machinery of any kind around, and it obviously hasn't been worked in many years. I think it is OK to collect here, but if there is any posting when you arrive, please obey it. If you are concerned, you might find someone in town who can help.

Opalite from the Eagle Picher mine pit. It is mostly white, with streaks of green and orange.

If you do collect here, you will have all kinds of fun. The floor and walls of the old pit are an opalite collector's dream. There are seams in the walls that seem to run forever. The exposed material is so dried out that it crumbles when hit, but if you do a little digging in the very soft soil, you will find some nice solid pieces. Even if you come away with only crumbled material, you will be able to enjoy its beautiful bright green fluorescence when you place the pieces under shortwave ultraviolet light.

Coal Canyon Road A: Dendrites

Land type: Mountains

Elevation: 4,500 feet

GPS: N40 02.13' / W118 07.90'

Best season: Spring through fall

Land manager: BLM

Material: Dendrites

Tools: Rock hammer

Vehicle: Any (provided the road is not wet)

Special attractions: None

Accommodations: Motels in Lovelock; RV parking and camping at Rye Patch State Recreation Area; open camping on BLM land

Finding the site: From Lovelock, drive north on I-80 for about 7 miles to the Coal Canyon exit. Go east on the blacktop Coal Canyon Road for 13.1 miles to the well-marked turnoff to Dago Pass. Drive north on the Dago Pass Road for 1.3 miles to a dirt road heading east. This dirt road was OK for cars driven slowly when I was there, but it looked as though it could be a real mess in wet weather. Follow this dirt road for 1.7 miles. At this point you will see an old mine with lots of tailings on your left. Drive as close as you can to it and park.

Some nice dendrites can be found near the old workings at Coal Canyon Road A, Site 18.

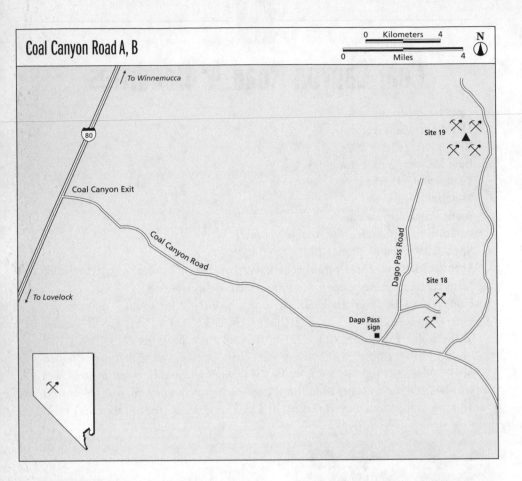

Coal Canyon Road A, B

0 Kilometers 4

0 Miles 4

N

To Winnemucca

80

Site 19

Coal Canyon Exit

Coal Canyon Road

Dago Pass Road

To Lovelock

Site 18

Dago Pass sign

Rockhounding

When my wife and I did the first edition, we found some nice pieces of white marble on the tailings. This time, there were only a very few. There were some nice dendrites, although they were not abundant. There are lots of old mines to explore in this area, though. If you live in New Jersey, I wouldn't suggest that you plan a trip to this area, but if you are driving on I-80 between Reno and Winnemucca and you have an hour or so to kill, this might be a little fun.

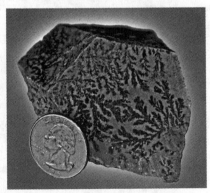

This nice dendrite is from Coal Canyon Road A.

Coal Canyon Road B: Dendrites, Mystery Material

See map on page 68.
Land type: Hills
Elevation: 4,300 feet
GPS: N40 07.74' / W118 10.06'
Best season: Spring and fall
Land manager: BLM
Material: Dendrites
Tools: Rock hammer
Vehicle: Any
Special attractions: None
Accommodations: Motels in Love-lock; RV parking and camping at Rye Patch State Recreation Area; open camping on BLM land
Finding the site: From the Dago Pass turnoff on Coal Canyon Road at Site 18, continue east on Coal Canyon Road for another 1.6 miles to a wide gravel road going north. Follow this road for 7 miles. At this point, there are low hills on both sides of the road. Park off the road and hunt in the hills and on the flats.

Rockhounding

For the first edition, we went to this site to find fossils. Our directions did not say what kind of fossils, which was OK since it turned out that I was the only fossil out there. We did find some really nice black dendrites

This 30 x 22 mm pendant is made from the "mystery material" from Coal Canyon Road B.

on a very white matrix. We also found some tiny cubes in a dark matrix. I believe the cubes are limonite pseudomorphs after pyrite.

For this edition, I was in a bit of a hurry, so I verified that there are still a few of the dendrites. I also have a feeling that there are fossils out there. There is a lot of area to explore, so if you have time, give it a try.

I also found some "mystery material." It is off-white with little brown freckles. It looks and cuts like marble, and takes a nice polish. The pieces are fairly small, but many will yield 30 x 40 mm cabs. Like Site 18, I would not recommend that you plan a trip just to this site, but if you are in the area, it is well worth a little exploring.

Unionville: Fossils

Land type: Mountains

Elevation: 4,924 feet (gate on Unionville Road); 5,124 feet (at the fork); 5,580 feet (at the gate before the parking area)

GPS: N40 26.77' / W118 06.91' (at the gate on Unionville Road); N40 26.49' / W118 07.48' (at the fork); N40 26.02' / W118 07.67' (at the gate before the parking area)

Best season: Spring through early fall

Land manager: BLM

Material: Fossils

Tools: Rock hammer

Vehicle: High clearance; four-wheel drive recommended

Special attractions: Many old mines in the area

Accommodations: Old Pioneer Garden Bed and Breakfast in Unionville; motels in Winnemucca

Finding the site: From Winnemucca, head south on I-80 for about 28 miles to exit 149. At the bottom of the ramp, turn left onto NV 400 and continue 16.6 miles to Unionville. If you have GPS, just set the coordinates to find the gate on the Unionville Road. If you don't have GPS, set your odometer at the Old

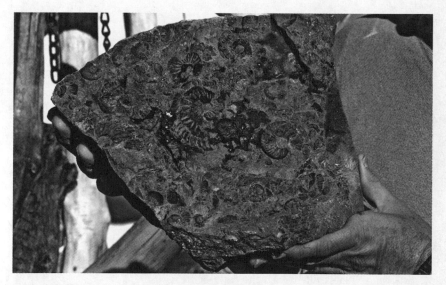

This beautiful fossil plate is from the Unionville site.

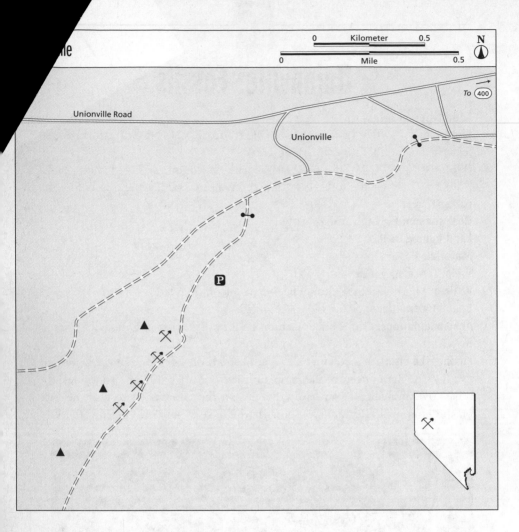

Pioneer Garden Bed and Breakfast and drive south for 0.4 mile to the gate on the right. From the gate, drive 0.6 mile to a fork. Take the left fork up the hill to a second gate. Park on the flat at the far side of the gate and hunt all along the shelf road ahead. If you have four-wheel drive, you can drive up the road, but there is no place to park and no place to turn around for a long way. It is far easier and more productive to hunt on foot.

Rockhounding

The main fossils here are ammonites, and there are some beauties. You can find individuals and plates filled with the little critters.

Cordero (McDermitt)
Opalite, Sulfur, Cinnabar

Land type: Desert
Elevation: 4,900 feet
GPS: N41 55.49' / W117 48.85'
Best season: Spring and fall
Land manager: BLM, private
Material: Cinnabar, opalite, sulfur crystals
Tools: Rock hammer
Vehicle: Any (to the end of the pavement)
Special attractions: The old Mercury mine
Accommodations: Motels in McDermitt; open camping on BLM land
Finding the site: From McDermitt, drive west on the only paved road out of town for 4.4 miles to a sign indicating the road to Disaster Peak. Keep left on the pavement for about 6 more miles to the mine. From this point on the road is dirt. Sometimes it is alright for any vehicle, and at other times it will require high clearance. It is only 0.5 mile or so to the tailings, so it is not a long walk, and you may find a lot of material that you wouldn't see from a vehicle.

Rockhounding

This was a very big operation in its day. There are old workings and relatively new ones. Much of the area is fenced and posted, so be sure to obey the signs. Don't worry, though,

A nice piece of opalite in shades of off-white and root beer brown from the Cordero Mine near McDermitt.

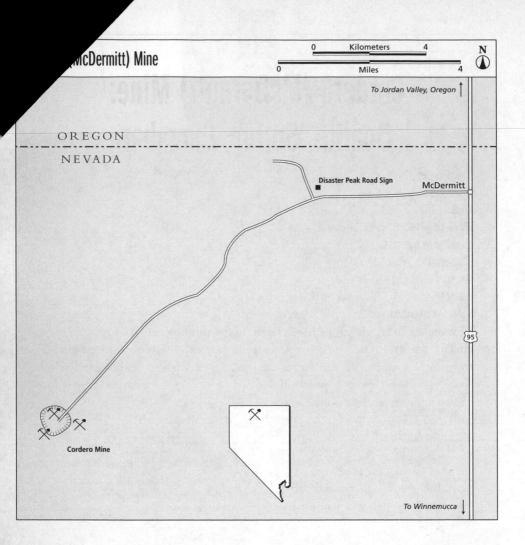

because there are still lots of tailings to poke around in, and all in all the area looks pretty much like it did when the first edition was researched. It is still not one of the premier collecting areas near McDermitt, but it is close to town and (mostly) on a blacktop road, so it would be a shame not to spend at least a little time here.

Agate Hill: Agate

Land type: Hills
Elevation: 5,200 feet
GPS: N42 01.50' / W117 51.98'
Best season: Spring and fall
Land manager: BLM
Material: Agate
Tools: Rock hammer
Vehicle: Any to the bottom of the hill; high clearance to the top
Special attractions: None
Accommodations: Motels in McDermitt; open camping on BLM land
Finding the site: From the Cordero Mine, drive back to the Disaster Peak sign. (*NOTE:* When researching the second edition, there was no sign when heading east, so keep an eye out for the sign on the westbound side of the road.) Take the dirt road toward Disaster Peak. As you turn onto the road, another

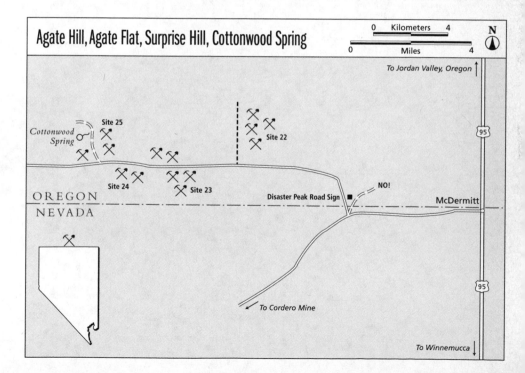

dirt road goes north. Stay to the left and continue toward Disaster Peak for 4 miles. At this point, a dirt track goes up the hill to the right just before the cattle guard. If you have a high-clearance vehicle, drive up the track 0.4 mile and park on the wide flat area at the top of the hill. If your vehicle won't make it, just hoof it up there. You will find agate all the way to the top. Thank your lucky stars that the way back is downhill, because you will have a bazillion pounds of agate to carry.

This agate with dendrites was found on Agate Hill, near McDermitt. Black dendrites are on white, tan, and brown agate.

Rockhounding

There is still agate all over the hills, and in the old pits where others have dug. Even though this is an old site, there is still plenty here.

Agate Flat: Agate, Petrified Wood

See map on page 75.
Land type: Flat desert
Elevation: 5,400 feet
GPS: N42 01.50' / W117 54.31'
Best season: Spring and fall
Land manager: BLM
Material: Agate, petrified wood
Tools: Rock hammer
Vehicle: Any
Special attractions: None
Accommodations: Motels in McDermitt; open camping on BLM land
Finding the site: From the cattle guard on the road to Disaster Peak (described in the directions for Site 22), drive 2.2 miles farther on the Disaster Peak road. Here you will see a large flat parking area on the left. Pull in and park anywhere.

Rockhounding

This is another old site that has been pretty well picked over, and you will have to do some roaming around the area to find the good stuff. There is still some left, but it won't run out and jump into your rock bag. The site is right next to the road, though, so at least you don't have to drive down 10 miles of washboard to get to it. Be sure to hunt on both sides of the road and even up the road that leads south out of the flat.

This agatized wood is from Agate Flat, near McDermitt.

Surprise Hill: Wood in Matrix, Mystery Stone

See map on page 75.
Land type: Hills
Elevation: 5,000 feet
GPS: N42 01.39' / W117 54.61'
Best season: Spring and fall
Land manager: BLM
Material: Petrified wood, mystery stone
Tools: Rock hammer, thin chisel or putty knife
Vehicle: Any (to the bottom of the hill)
Special attractions: None
Accommodations: Motels in McDermitt; open camping on BLM land
Finding the site: From Site 23, go 0.6 mile west on the Disaster Peak road. At this point, you will see some yellowish rock and evidence of a lot of digging on a hill to the left. Some ruts go up the hill to the rocks, but you will need at least a high-clearance vehicle to reach them. It is only about 0.1 mile to the site, though, so if you must, just park off the road and walk up the ruts.

Rockhounding

One of the nice things about writing books like this is that you can name the sites just about anything you want. Obviously, this little hill has no name on any maps, so I named it Surprise Hill. The name is in honor of the surprise I got when I first hunted here.

When we were gathering material for the first edition, Cora and I were on our way back from

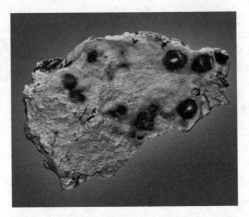

These agate eyes are from the Surprise Hill site.

Petrified wood specimens from Surprise Hill.

a trip to the Disaster Peak wonderstone site and were just puttering along looking for possibilities. I had looked at the hill on the way out and decided that it probably had more of the same stuff as Agate Flat. On a whim I decided to see if that was true. I popped in the four-wheel drive, grunted up to the rocks, and parked. It was cold and the wind was blowing as we started looking around. The rocks looked as though they had been hunted in, but I didn't see a sign of anything. Cora was down below and found a few nice pieces of wood, but I was getting skunked. Just as I was about to give in to the wind and cold and head for lunch, I picked up a softball-size hunk of yellow rock, and lo and behold, there was a beautiful piece of silicified wood encased in the rock. A little searching turned up quite a few small but really well-defined pieces in this yellowish matrix. They make really great displays, so if you get to the McDermitt area, be sure to see where I got my surprise. Maybe you will get one too.

For the second edition I did not take time to break up a lot of the yellow rock, but it is still there. I did discover that my name for the hill was correct, since this time I found yet another surprise. This consisted of groups of black agatized eyes with a tiny dot of white in the center encased in a fairly soft white matrix. When I get some time, I'll try to get it identified, but for now, I'll just call it mystery rock. If you find some and know what it is, let me know.

Cottonwood Spring: Opalized Wood

See map on page 75.

Land type: Hills
Elevation: 4,900 feet
GPS: N42 01.64' / W117 55.59'
Best season: Spring and fall
Land manager: BLM
Material: Opalized wood
Tools: Rock hammer
Vehicle: Any
Special attractions: None
Accommodations: Motels in McDermitt; open camping on BLM land
Finding the site: From the turnoff to Site 24, continue west on Disaster Peak Road for 0.8 mile to a dirt road heading north. Take this road about 0.2 mile to the wide parking and camping area at the bottom of the hill. Park here and hunt on the hills in all directions.

Rockhounding

There is a lot of opalized wood in this area, but you will have to do some walking and stooping. I found some nice pieces on the uphill slope on the east side of the road and on the downhill slope on the west side. A little digging probably won't hurt either.

Opalized wood from Cottonwood Spring near McDermitt. Colors are predominantly white and green.

Opal Wood Hill: Opalized Wood

Land type: Hills
Elevation: 5,400 feet
GPS: N42 03.58' / W117 56.75'
Best season: Spring and fall
Land manager: BLM
Material: Opalized wood
Tools: Rock hammer
Vehicle: High clearance
Special attractions: None
Accommodations: Motels in McDermitt; open camping on BLM land

The whole hillside at Opal Wood Hill (Site 26) is covered with opalized wood.

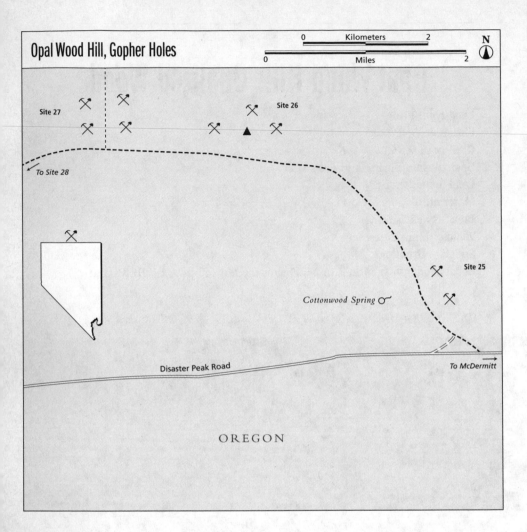

Finding the site: From Site 25, drive 2.6 miles on the rough dirt road heading north from the Disaster Peak road. This road is usually OK for high-clearance vehicles, but I would not recommend trying it in a passenger car. At the 2.6-mile spot, you will see a white hill on the right with some tracks going up the slope. If you have a four-wheel drive, you can drive to the top, but it is rough and not really necessary. In fact, you may find more material by hiking up the tracks.

Rockhounding

This is another interesting spot. There is a ton of opalized wood on the road to the top of the hill. A lot of digging has been done on the sides of the hill, and you can hunt in these little pits to see what is available. Roam all over the hill and in the flats below to get the best material. You might want to create your own hole in the ground and find some premium stuff. Who knows? There is a lot of territory to cover, so I hope you brought your lunch.

I hope you brought your ultraviolet lamp along too. If you did, you will be able to see nice orange and green fluorescence in the wood under long-wave light.

Black, brown, and white opalized wood from Opal Wood Hill.

Gopher Holes: Agatized and Opalized Wood

See map on page 82.
Land type: Hills
Elevation: 5,400 feet
GPS: N42 03.70' / W117 57.71'
Best season: Spring and fall
Land manager: BLM
Material: Agatized and opalized wood
Tools: Rock hammer, pick, and shovel (bulldozer)
Vehicle: High clearance
Special attractions: None
Accommodations: Motels in McDermitt; open camping on BLM land
Finding the site: From Site 26, continue west on the dirt road for 1.2 miles. At this point, a dirt track goes north. When the site was researched for the first edition, overexuberant diggers had dug holes right in the road so that it was only possible to drive up the dirt road a few feet. Visiting for the second edition, I found that the holes and the material were still there, but the road had been snaked around the holes and continued a long way out to the hills. I didn't have time to follow the road, but I'll bet there is more wood out there.

Rockhounding

This is another place where I took it upon myself to invent a name. Since so many people have dug pits here, it looks like the land of the super gophers. It is also a super place for collecting agatized and opalized wood. You will find so many nice pieces in and around the pits that you really will not have to do any digging. What you will do is look at the beautiful material that others have left and drool about what they must have taken with them.

When you finish drooling, shine your long-wave ultraviolet lamp on the wood samples and enjoy the green and orange fluorescence.

A very nice piece of agatized wood from Gopher Holes, near McDermitt. Colors are tan and brown.

Red Tailings: Opalite

Land type: Hills
Elevation: 5,200 feet
GPS: N42 02.99' / W118 02.16'
Best season: Spring and fall
Land manager: BLM
Material: Opalite
Tools: Rock hammer
Vehicle: High clearance
Special attractions: None
Accommodations: Motels in McDermitt; open camping on BLM land
Finding the site: There are two ways to get to this site, and you will have to decide which is best for you. If you start from Site 27, you can continue west on the dirt road for 5.4 miles to the site, a big old mine with three tailings piles, one of which is dark red. The problem with this route, however, is that the 5.4 miles may seem more like 50 miles. The road is in about the same condition as

The pit at the "opalite mine," Site 28, is full of nice pieces of opalite in a variety of colors.

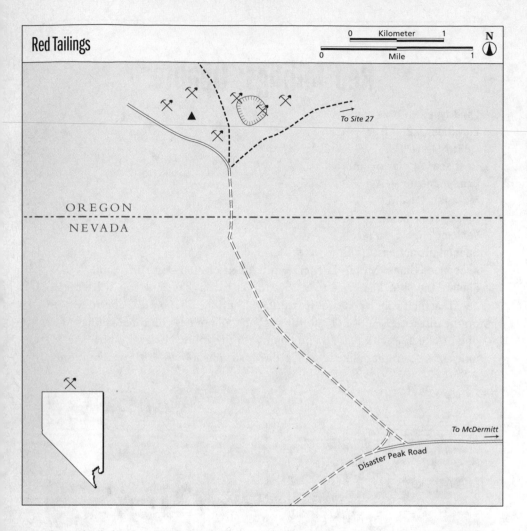

that which leads to Site 27, so if you didn't mind a few "gopher holes," keep going. I happen to hate crawling along over rocks at a couple of miles an hour, and if you feel the same, you might want to try the second route.

For the second route, follow the first route to Disaster Peak Road. Go west on Disaster Peak Road for 5.5 miles to a road going right. Follow this road for 2 miles to a fork. The left fork goes down to the tailings, and the right fork goes to the mine. You will want to hunt in both places, so take your choice as to which one to do first.

Be aware that there are a number of roads in this area, and it can get a little confusing. The key is to keep heading for the red tailings. If you can't see the tailings, you are on the wrong road. Even if you take a wrong turn, it is easily corrected by turning around and giving it another shot. This is a perfect place for GPS navigation.

Rockhounding

When I was here researching the second edition, there was a DO NOT ENTER sign at the mine, and another sign saying that Oregon had designated this for cleanup. It is impossible to say what the

Opalite from Red Tailings, Site 28.

status will be by the time you get this book and decide to head out there. I'm leaving it in because it is a great site. There are tons of nice opalite here, both on the tailings and in the old mine pit. Be sure you take the time to hunt all over the area. There has been some green jasper reported along the road northwest of the mine pit, but I didn't find any. You might. Save me some. Much of the opalite from this spot will fluoresce orange and green under both long- and shortwave ultraviolet light.

...he Pit: Picture Stone

Best season: Spring and fall
Land manager: BLM
Material: Picture stone
Tools: Rock hammer and/or heavy digging tools
Vehicle: Any
Special attractions: None
Accommodations: Motels in McDermitt; open camping on BLM land
Finding the site: From the turnoff to Cottonwood Spring (Site 25), continue 7.2 miles on Disaster Peak Road to the easily seen diggings on the left. Drive up the dirt road for a hundred yards or so and park.

Rockhounding

I was on my way to check out the wonderstone out on Disaster Peak Road when I saw some diggings off to the left. I took a look and discovered picture

There is a lot of picture stone like this at Site 29.

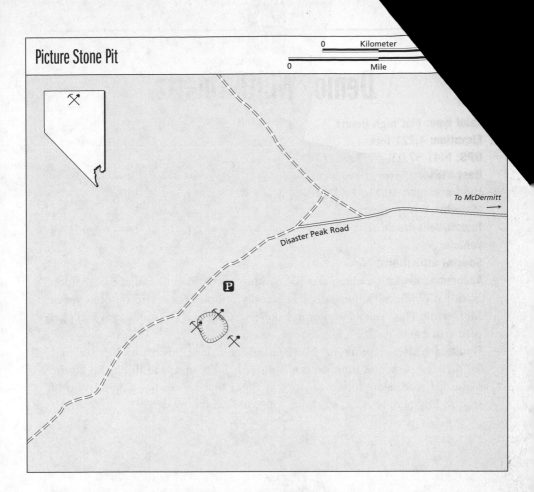

Picture Stone Pit

0   Kilometer

0   Mile

To McDermitt

Disaster Peak Road

P

stone. There were lots of small to medium pieces all around and in the pit. If you should want something bigger, attack the pit wall with gusto and you won't have to go to the gym for a month. By the way, I had been driving since about 9 a.m., and at 3:30 p.m. I arrived at the spot where the wonderstone quarry had been. Just as I was thinking that I was in the wrong spot, the first vehicle I had seen all day came by and the driver solved our problem. It seems that a couple of years ago, the rancher had filled in the pit. I guess it was hazard to his cattle. Well, the picture stone is prettier, and it is closer, too.

: White Quartz

W118 40.72'

season: Spring through fall

Land manager: BLM

Material: White quartz

Tools: Rock hammer

Vehicle: Any

Special attractions: None

Accommodations: Camping and RV parking on BLM land and at the Sheldon National Wildlife Refuge. This area is really remote. The nearest motels are in McDermitt (110 miles away) or in Lakeview, Oregon (117 miles away), so plan your trip carefully.

Finding the site: Traveling on NV 292 in Denio, take this main dirt road west for 4 miles, park, and hunt on both sides of the road. If the directions to the main dirt road seem a little vague, remember that Denio has a population of around fifty people . . . so trust me, you will find the road.

Malachite on white quartz from Denio Junction.

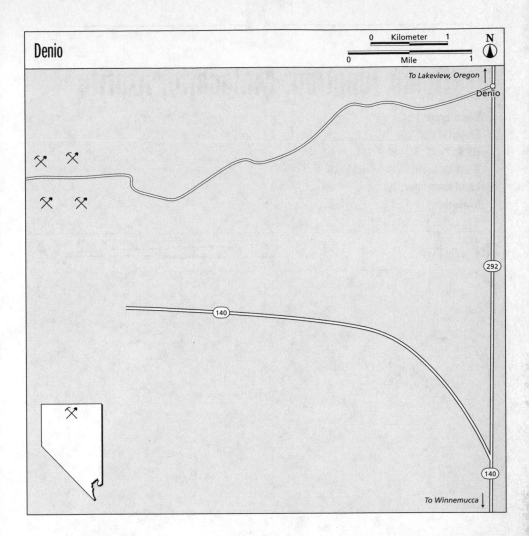

0   Kilometer   1

0   Mile   1

N

To Lakeview, Oregon ↑

Denio

292

140

140

To Winnemucca ↓

Rockhounding

The white quartz here is plentiful and pretty, but unless you have a burning desire for white quartz, I wouldn't recommend that you plan a trip from New Jersey just to visit this site. On the other hand, if you have just spent hours on NV 140, this is a short detour and a chance to stretch your legs and get some pretty stones in the bargain.

Denio Junction: Malachite, Azurite

Land type: Hills
Elevation: 4,400 feet
GPS: N41 56.98' / W118 42.48'
Best season: Spring and fall
Land manager: BLM
Material: Malachite, azurite on quartz

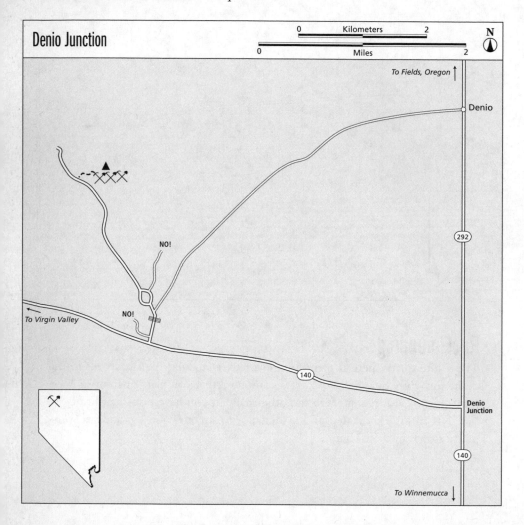

Denio Junction

The old mine at Denio Junction will yield a lot of nice mineral samples.

Tools: Rock hammer
Vehicle: High clearance
Special attractions: None
Accommodations: Camping and RV parking on BLM land and at the Sheldon National Wildlife Refuge
Finding the site: From Denio Junction, drive west on NV 140 for 2.9 miles to a dirt road heading northeast. Turn onto the road, cross the cattle guard, and go left at the fork. Follow the left fork for 1.5 miles, to where a dirt track goes 0.1 mile to the easily seen mine.

Rockhounding

In the first edition, I wrote: "This is a nice spot to take a break from the boredom of miles and miles of NV 140. I recommend high-clearance vehicles to the site, but I'm sure some of you will take a car there. You be the judge. If the weather is nice and you are a hiker, you might even want to walk. Who knows what you might find along the way. The site is only 1.5 miles from the highway and has some nice specimens of malachite and azurite on white quartz. We also found some pretty selenite crystals. If you are a mineral collector, you will probably find things I walked over."

I can't think of anything better to say today. This is still a nifty little site for mineral specimens. One caution is to keep an eye on the little ones. There is a very deep shaft with a good fence around it, but some will want to climb it. The shaft is open and holds a great fascination for the kids.

If you have some extra time and energy, there are several other mines in the area, some of which can be seen from this site. Do you suppose they have the same material as this one? Or is it even better? Maybe you had better go and see.

SITE
32

Virgin Valley Turnoff: Apache Tears, Obsidian, Chalcedony

Land type: Low hills
Elevation: 4,900 feet
GPS: N41 52.60' / W119 01.66'

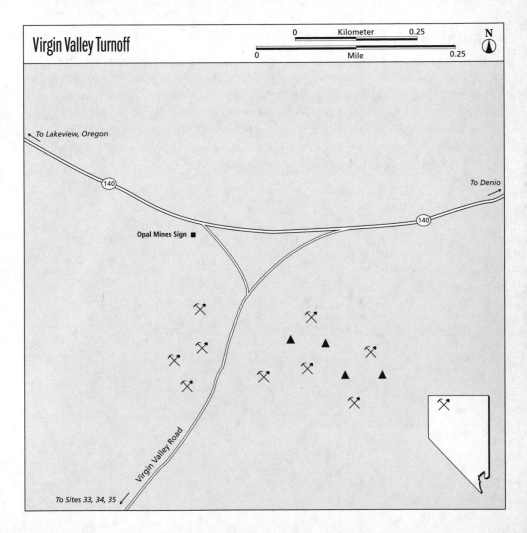

Best season: Spring through fall

Land manager: BLM

Material: Apache tears, obsidian nodules, chalcedony

Tools: Rock hammer

Vehicle: Any

Special attractions: Sheldon National Wildlife Refuge

Accommodations: RV parking and camping at Sheldon National Wildlife Refuge; open camping on BLM land

Finding the site: From Denio Junction, go west on NV 140 for 25.1 miles to the Virgin Valley turnoff. The turnoff is marked with a sign to the opal mines. Turn onto the graded road and park anywhere off the road.

Rockhounding

There is a lot of different material out here, but except for the tears, the chalcedony, and the obsidian nodules, it is widely scattered and scarce. If you spend a lot of time you will probably find opalite, maybe some opal, some petrified wood, and maybe a little agate. Roam all over the low hills and in the washes on both sides of the road. You definitely will find the obsidian and the chalcedony, and you may get lucky with some of the other. Some of the chalcedony will fluoresce green under shortwave ultraviolet light.

Royal Peacock Mine: Precious Opal

Land type: Hills

Elevation: 4,900 feet

GPS: N41 52.60' / W119 01.66' (taken at the turnoff from NV 140)

Best season: May 15 through Oct 15 (as of 2010)

Land manager: Private; fee to dig

Material: Precious opal

Tools: Short-handled, sharp-pointed pick, shovel or garden rake, screwdriver with 8"-long blade ground to a point, ice pick or similar tool, small bucketlike container, plastic containers, zipper storage bags, gloves, squirt bottle, kneeling pad, hat, and sunscreen

Vehicle: Any

Special attractions: Sheldon National Wildlife Refuge

Accommodations: Two furnished trailers at the site (reservations required); RV parking with full hookups (reservations suggested); tent space; restroom and laundry room. No-fee camping at Sheldon Wildlife Refuge. Motels in McDermitt.

Finding the site: Signs will guide you to the mine. From Lakeview, Oregon, drive 84.4 miles on OR 140/NV 140 to the well-marked Virgin Valley turnoff. From Winnemucca, drive north on US 95 for 32.5 miles to NV 140. Go northwest on NV 140 for 65.3 miles. At Denio Junction, keep left on NV 140 for 25.1 miles to the Virgin Valley turnoff. Follow the Virgin Valley Road to the Royal Peacock Mine. The road is well marked and the numerous signs will ensure that you will not get lost.

Cora chats with some folks looking for the "Hope Opal" at the Royal Peacock Opal Mine.

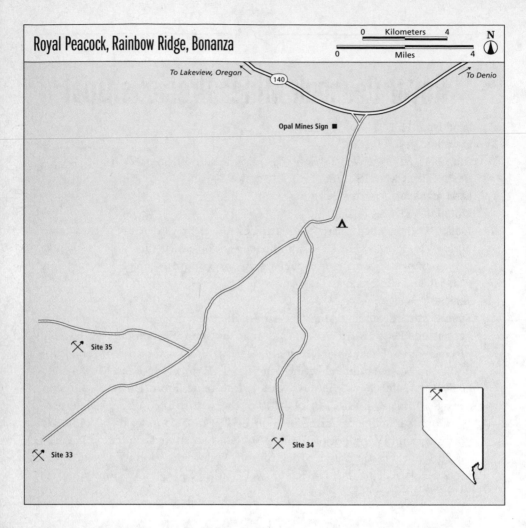

Royal Peacock, Rainbow Ridge, Bonanza

0   Kilometers   4

0   Miles   4

N

To Lakeview, Oregon   140   To Denio

Opal Mines Sign ■

Site 35

Site 33

Site 34

Rockhounding

Here you must pay a fee to dig for precious opal. There is one fee for digging in the tailings and a higher fee for digging in the mine walls. Obviously, there is a much greater chance of finding a large opal in the wall than in the tailings—hence the higher fee. If you are an opalholic, you will surely want to try this kind of hunting. The fee will be small in comparison to the retail price if you find a really nice stone.

It is strongly recommended that you call first for reservations. This is a long way from anywhere, and you wouldn't want to arrive and find there are no accommodation vacancies. You can reach the mine operators at Royal Peacock Mine, P.O. Box 165, Denio, NV 89404; (775) 941-0374; www.royalpeacock.com.

Rainbow Ridge Opal Mine: Precious Opal

See map on page 98.
Land type: Hills
Elevation: 4,900 feet
GPS: N41 52.60' / W119 01.66' (taken at the turnoff from NV 140)
Best season: May 28 through Sept 19 (closed Wed and Thurs in 2010)
Land manager: Private; fee to dig
Material: Precious opal
Tools: Small pick, small garden rake, small shovel or trowel, spray bottle, five-gallon buckets (plus one extra for seat), sunscreen, hat, and gloves
Vehicle: Any
Special attractions: Sheldon National Wildlife Refuge
Accommodations: RV parking and camping at the Sheldon National Wildlife Refuge; open camping on BLM land; motel in McDermitt
Finding the site: The way is well signed. From Lakeview, Oregon, drive 84.4 miles on OR 140/NV 140 to the well-marked Virgin Valley turnoff. From Winnemucca, drive north on US 95 for 32.5 miles to NV 140. Go northwest on NV 140 for 65.3 miles. At Denio Junction, keep left on NV 140 for 25.1 miles to the Virgin Valley turnoff. Follow the Virgin Valley Road to the Rainbow Ridge Mine. The road is well marked and the numerous signs will ensure that you will not get lost.

Rockhounding

Rainbow Ridge is another fee-to-dig site, but here the digging is limited to the tailings or to loads from the mine that have been spread and leveled off. Nevertheless, some beautiful opal has been found here, and if you are a careful searcher, you will probably come out on the plus side financially. Plus, you won't have to do the heavy digging. The gift shop is filled with beautiful specimens from the area, and you can forego the searching and just search your wallet to pay for your specimens.

It is strongly recommended that you write or phone before coming way out here. It would be a long drive only to find out that for some reason the mine was closed. You can reach the owners, Glen and Donna Hodson, at Rainbow Ridge Opal Mine, Box 97, Denio, NV 89404; (775) 941-0270 (Apr through Oct), (541) 548-4810 (Nov through Mar); glen@nevadaopal.com; www.nevadaopal.com.

Bonanza Opal Mines: Precious Opal

See map on page 98.

Land type: Hills

Elevation: 4,900 feet

GPS: N41 52.60' / W119 01.66' (taken at the turnoff from NV 140)

Best season: May 20 through Sept 30 (as of 2010)

Land manager: Private; fee to dig

Material: Precious opal

Tools: Water bottles, small rake, spray bottle, buckets for specimens, folding chair, sunscreen, hat, and gloves

Vehicle: Any

Special attractions: Sheldon National Wildlife Refuge

Accommodations: RV parking and camping at the Sheldon National Wildlife Refuge; open camping on BLM land, motels in McDermitt

Finding the site: Signs will guide you to the mine. From Lakeview, Oregon, drive 84.4 miles on OR 140/NV 140 to the well-marked Virgin Valley turnoff. From Winnemucca, drive north on US 95 for 32.5 miles to NV 140. Go northwest on NV 140 for 65.3 miles. At Denio Junction, keep left on NV 140 for 25.1 miles to the Virgin Valley turnoff. Follow the Virgin Valley Road to the Bonanza mines. The road is well marked and the numerous signs will ensure that you will not get lost.

Rockhounding

The folks at the Bonanza let the fee diggers work in material they have removed in their regular mining operations. It has not been screened, which means they have not taken out all of the good stuff. People find opalized limb sections, opalized pine cones, and other prehistoric organic material here. One day in 1973, while scraping the area for visiros, the bulldozer blade flipped up what Keith Hodson thought was a bottle. Unfortunately, instead of a bottle, it was just a six-pound opal filled with flashes of fire. Do I have your attention yet? To find out how to get here and start looking for your "bottle," try contacting the mine at (864) 597–1421; info@bonanzaopals.com; www.bonanzaopals.net.

Gooch Spring: Obsidian

Land type: Hills; high desert
Elevation: 5,952 feet
GPS: N41 53.14' / W119 16.75'
Best season: Spring and fall
Land manager: Sheldon National Wildlife Reserve
Material: Obsidian

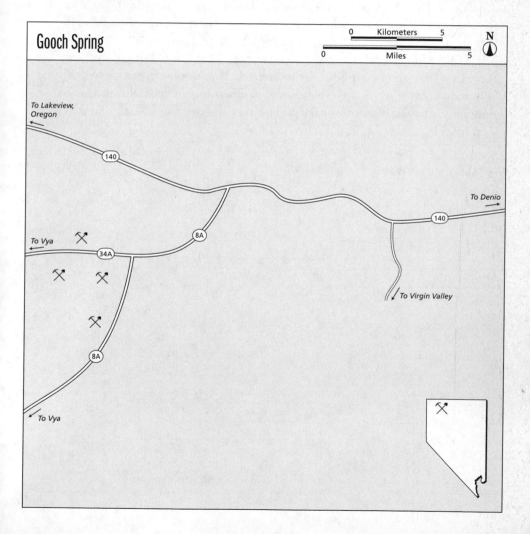

Tools: Rock hammer
Vehicle: Any
Special attractions: Wildlife viewing
Accommodations: RV parking and camping at Sheldon National Wildlife Refuge; open camping on BLM land
Finding the site: From the Virgin Valley Turnoff (Site 32), drive 9.9 miles to NV 8A, going left. Continue down NV 8A for 5 miles to a fork where NV 34A goes right. Park here and hunt between the forks and all around the area.

Rockhounding

This site is literally packed with obsidian. There is everything from tears to fist-size nodules. Most is black, but I found several nice mahogany nodules. If you are a fan of dirt road driving, you can continue down either NV 8A or NV 34A, and in around 35 or 40 miles, you will be at the old site of Vya and the start of the sites down NV 34A to Gerlach. If not, you can return to NV 140 and continue on to Lakeview, Oregon, down to Alturas, California, and through Cedarville, California, to Vya. This way is farther and lonely, but it is a pretty ride.

Vya: Obsidian

Land type: Flat, high desert
Elevation: 5,732 feet
GPS: N41 22.06' / W119 38.28'
Best season: Spring and fall
Land manager: BLM
Material: Obsidian

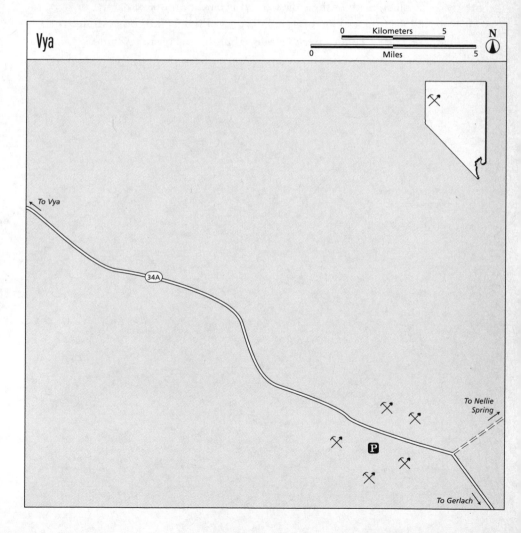

Tools: Rock hammer
Vehicle: Any
Special attractions: None
Accommodations: Motels in Cedarville and Alturas, CA; one motel in Gerlach, NV; dry camping and RV parking on BLM land
Finding the site: From the junction of NV 8A and NV 34A at Vya, drive south on NV 34A, for 19.3 miles. Park and hunt on both sides of the road.

Rockhounding

I know that this site is almost 20 miles from Vya, and I know that Vya exists mostly in our imaginations these days, but it is hard to think of names for sites out here, and Vya sounds kind of neat. Don't you think? Hunt on both sides of the road, but don't take too much, because there is lots more to come.

Nellie Spring A: Opalite

Land type: Desert, hills
Elevation: 5,800 feet
GPS: N41 23.58' / W119 31.98'
Best season: Spring and fall
Land manager: BLM
Material: Opalite
Tools: Rock hammer, heavy hammers, chisels
Vehicle: High clearance; four-wheel drive recommended
Special attractions: None
Accommodations: Motels in Cedarville and Alturas, CA; motel in Gerlach, NV; open camping on BLM land
Finding the site: From Cedarville, CA, drive east on CA 299 for 20 miles (CA 299 becomes NV 8A at the border). At this point, NV 34 goes south toward Gerlach. Follow this road for 21 miles to a dirt road going left. (There used to be a sign to Nellie Spring here, but when researching for the second edition, it was gone.) Turn left on the dirt road and drive 2 miles. At this point, there will be a large flat area with a big metal water tank at the end. At the far end of the flat, take the road to the right and drive 3.4 miles, where a dirt track goes right about 0.3 mile to the site. This track is just before a cattle guard, so if you've crossed one, you just missed the track.

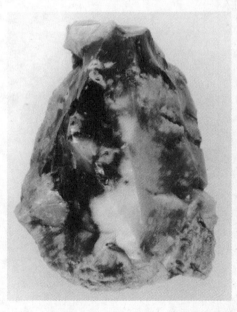

Rockhounding

There are opalite chips in a variety of colors all over the bottom of the old pit, and much of the material here will fluoresce

Black, white, and brown opalite from Nellie Spring A (Site 38).

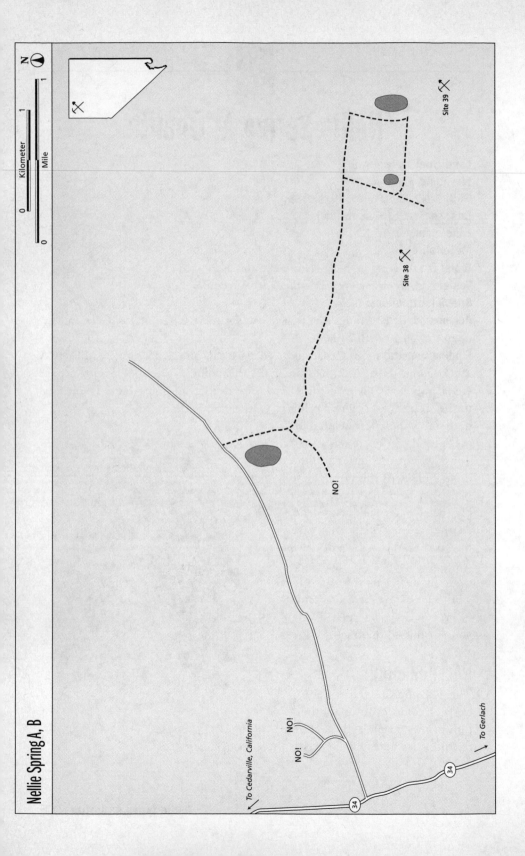

Nellie Spring A, B

From the size of the diggings, it looks like someone did some serious rockhounding at Nellie Spring A (Site 38).

green under shortwave ultraviolet light. In the bottom of the pit are several boulders of opalite. If you are not satisfied with the pieces you find, get out the heavy hammer and the chisels and go to work on the boulders. Be sure to wear eye protection. You don't want to take your opalite home in your eye. Besides, it is two-hundred million miles to a doctor from out here. In fact, this place reminds me of a T-shirt I once saw that said that (blank) may not be the end of the world, but you could see it from there.

NOTE: I have to admit that this was a very frustrating site to find for the second edition. The roads were completely different, the little earthen dam was gone, and tracks went off everywhere. Once I found the way, however, it was fairly simple. But I can't say strongly enough that a GPS is worth its weight in gold out here. Not only will it get you to the site, but it will get you back. This is really the back side of beyond, and you might have to wait until politicians turn honest before someone happens along to help you.

Nellie Spring B: Opalite

See map on page 106.

Land type: Desert, hills
Elevation: 5,800 feet
GPS: N41 23.57' / W119 31.27'
Best season: Spring and fall
Land manager: BLM
Material: Opalite
Tools: Rock hammer
Vehicle: High clearance; four-wheel drive recommended

There is still a lot of opalite left at Nellie Spring B.

Special attractions: None

Accommodations: Motels in Cedarville and Alturas, CA; motel in Gerlach, NV; open camping on BLM land

Finding the site: From Nellie Spring A, a dirt track goes up behind the pit and across the desert. Follow this track for about 0.5 mile to some very large diggings. You can't miss them, as they are visible for miles. Park near the piles and hunt all over the area. If this track looks a little rough to you, just go back to the road, turn right, cross the cattle guard, and drive about 0.5 mile to a track going over to the big tailings piles.

Rockhounding

This site is not as productive as Nellie Spring A, but a lot can be found by roaming over the hills and flats. If the sun is right, the ground twinkles with reflections from the opalite chips. While you are in this area, be sure to cover a lot of ground. You will see lots of little side roads and tracks, and lots of signs of digging. Give them a look. You just might find some museum-quality opalite. At the least, you will find some more chips that will fluoresce green under shortwave ultraviolet light.

Route 34–Cattle Guard: Obsidian, Apache Tears

Land type: Desert, hills
Elevation: 6,200 feet
GPS: N41 16.67' / W119 34.32'
Best season: Spring and fall
Land manager: BLM
Material: Obsidian nodules
Tools: Rock hammer
Vehicle: Any
Special attractions: None
Accommodations: Motels in Cedarville and Alturas, CA; motel in Gerlach, NV; open camping on BLM land

This nice little fossil plate is from the Cattle Guard site on Route 34.

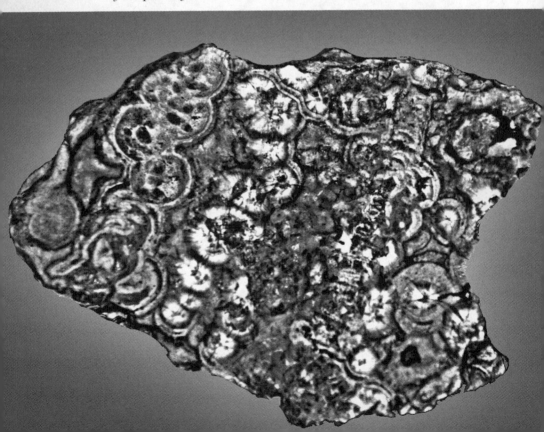

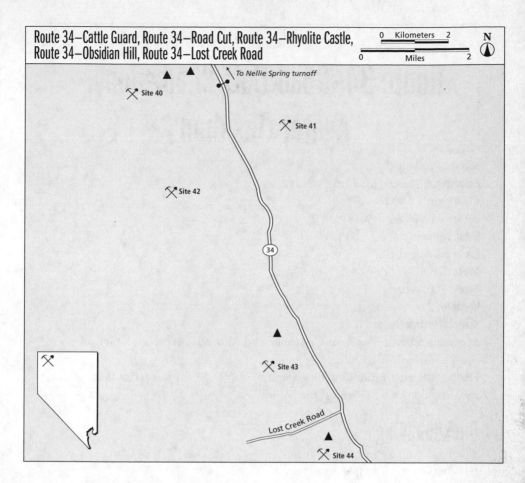

Kilometers

Miles

N

To Nellie Spring turnoff

Site 40

Site 41

Site 42

34

Site 43

Lost Creek Road

Site 44

Finding the site: From the Nellie Spring turnoff, proceed south on NV 34 for 5.9 miles to a cattle guard. Park in the wide area north of the cattle guard and hunt on both sides of the road.

Rockhounding

There is a fair amount of obsidian at this site. I had my best luck north of the cattle guard, but if you have the time, be sure to hunt all over the area. Pay particular attention to the slopes of the nearby hills. Even if you do not find the mother of all obsidian nodules, this is a good place to eat that sandwich you bought at the Nellie Spring Burger King.

Route 34-Road Cut: Chalcedony, Agate, Obsidian

See map on page 111.
Land type: Desert, road cut
Elevation: 6,100 feet
GPS: N41 16.36' / W119 34.20'
Best season: Spring and fall
Land manager: BLM
Material: Chalcedony, agate, obsidian
Tools: Rock hammer
Vehicle: Any
Special attractions: None
Accommodations: Motels in Cedarville and Alturas, CA; motel in Gerlach, NV; open camping on BLM land
Finding the site: From Site 40, go south on NV 34 for just 0.6 mile to a long road cut on the left. Park off the road.

Rockhounding

The road cut has a variety of material that a lot of people have been looking for, judging by the number of broken rocks. I found a lot of small pieces of a bubbly chalcedony in some pretty colors mixed with clear and white. This material fluoresces a nice pale green under shortwave ultraviolet light. I also found a few nice pieces of an amethyst-colored agate. I only found a little, but who knows what will be waiting after a nice rain? If you cross to the west side of the road, you can find some nice obsidian nodules.

Fluorescent chalcedony from the Road Cut site along Route 34.

Route 34-Rhyolite Castle: Obsidian

See map on page 111.
Land type: Desert, hills
Elevation: 5,700 feet
GPS: N41 15.25' / W119 33.47'
Best season: Spring and fall
Land manager: BLM
Material: Obsidian, petrified wood
Tools: Rock hammer
Vehicle: Any
Special attractions: None
Accommodations: Motels in Cedarville and Alturas, CA; motel in Gerlach, NV; open camping on BLM land

Obsidian and a little jasper can be found at the Rhyolite Castle on Route 34.

Finding the site: From Site 41, drive south on NV 34 for 1.2 miles. At this point, you will see some rhyolite pinnacles on the right. Dirt tracks lead to them in a couple of places. Take any of the tracks and park near the pinnacles.

Rockhounding

This is an interesting old hunting area. There is even an old tin shack built up against a rock wall on the back side of one of the pinnacles. I have no idea who lived there or why. You might be able to pick it up for a song. No more noisy neighbors.

Again, there is a lot of obsidian here. I found some very nicely defined silicified wood, but it is scarce. Other materials have been reported here, so spend a little time and wander out to both the east and the west. Some of the material from this site showed bright green fluorescent spots under shortwave ultraviolet light.

Petrified wood and fluorescent chalcedony from along Route 34.

Route 34–Obsidian Hill: Obsidian

See map on page 111.
Land type: Desert, hills
Elevation: 5,300 feet
GPS: N41 14.17' / W119 31.03'
Best season: Spring and fall
Land manager: BLM
Material: Obsidian
Tools: Rock hammer
Vehicle: Any
Special attractions: None
Accommodations: Motels in Cedarville and Alturas, CA; motel in Gerlach, NV;
open camping on BLM land

There is a lot of nice material on this low hill.

Finding the site: From Site 42, continue south on NV 34 for 2.5 miles to where a road used to go right. The access has been blocked, but if you look carefully, you can see the track. Just south of this track is a low hill a hundred yards or so from NV 34. Park off the road and hunt on the flats and slopes.

Rockhounding

There is good obsidian all the way from where you park to the top of the hill. Your problem will be in deciding which pieces to take and which to leave for me. Keep an eye out for occasional pieces of petrified wood and opalite.

Fluorescent chalcedony from Obsidian Hill.

Route 34–Lost Creek Road: Obsidian

See map on page 111.
Land type: Desert, hills
Elevation: 5,300 feet
GPS: N41 13.16' / W119 28.79'
Best season: Spring and fall
Land manager: BLM
Material: Obsidian
Tools: Rock hammer
Vehicle: Any
Special attractions: None
Accommodations: Motels in Cedarville and Alturas, CA; motel in Gerlach, NV; open camping on BLM land
Finding the site: From Site 43, continue south on NV 34 for 2.3 miles to the intersection with Lost Creek Road. Here you will see a white hill on the southwest side of the intersection. Park near the base and hunt on and around the hill.

Rockhounding

Once again, you will find lots of obsidian without really trying. Or, if you're really diligent, you may find some petrified wood and maybe a little agate and/or opalite.

This hill at the turn to Lost Creek Road is a prime spot for obsidian.

Pioche: Calcite Crystals

Land type: Mountains
Elevation: 6,400 feet
GPS: N38 5.79' / W114 35.71'
Best season: Spring and fall
Land manager: BLM
Material: Calcite crystals
Tools: Rock hammer
Vehicle: High clearance
Special attractions: Pioche Historic Area
Accommodations: Motels in Pioche; RV parking and camping at Echo Canyon
State Recreational Area; open camping on BLM land

The road to the Pioche site is rough, but it is worth it if you can make it.

Finding the site: From the intersection of NV 322 and US 93 at Pioche, drive north on US 93 for 13.4 miles and turn onto a graded road going left. Immediately after the turn, a rough track heads left up the hill. Follow the track for 0.8 mile to the mine dumps. This track has deteriorated significantly since the first edition, and now definitely requires at least a high-clearance vehicle.

Rockhounding

Search around the dumps for some nice white calcite crystals on a black matrix. There are several kinds of mineral samples to be had here, and some of them fluoresce a pretty pink under shortwave ultraviolet light.

White calcite crystals on black matrix from the Pioche site.

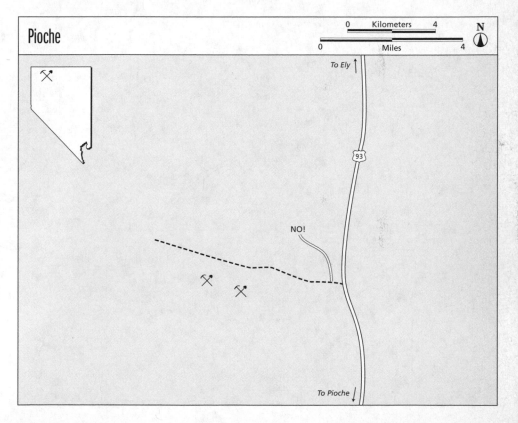

Major's Place: Calcite

Land type: Road cut
Elevation: 6,800 feet
GPS: N 39 2.30' / W114 36.46'
Best season: Spring through fall
Land manager: Nevada Department of Transportation

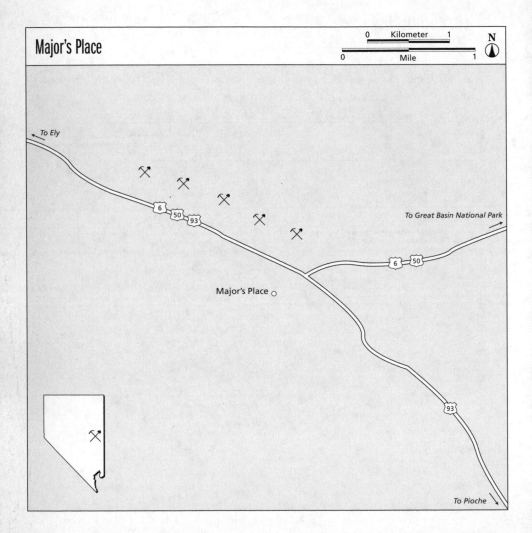

Material: Calcite
Tools: Rock hammer
Vehicle: Any
Special attractions: Historic Ward Charcoal Ovens; Cave Lake State Recreation Area; Great Basin National Park
Accommodations: Motels in Ely and Baker; RV parking and camping in Ely, Great Basin National Park, Cave Lake State Recreation Area, and Baker
Finding the site: From the intersection of US 93 and US 50 at Major's Place, go north on US 93/50 toward Ely. The road cut starts just north of the intersection and extends for about 2 miles. Safe parking places are scarce, so you will have to do a little walking to explore the whole cut.

Rockhounding

This is the place that got me interested in looking for fluorescent minerals. I had some old information that said there was fluorescent calcite in the long road cut. I got there and found lots of nice big pieces of clear to white calcite and took it home to check out under an ultraviolet lamp. But when I got home, got a lamp, and checked it out, guess what? No fluorescence! Oh well, the calcite is still nice, so be sure to stop and pick some up. There is probably some there that will fluoresce, and you just may pick some up. Good luck.

Garnet Hill: Garnets

Land type: Mountains
Elevation: 7,200 feet
GPS: N39 16.93' / W114 56.93'
Best season: Spring through fall
Land manager: BLM
Material: Garnet
Tools: Small digging tools, screen
Vehicle: Any
Special attractions: Cave Lake State Recreation Area; open pit copper mine at Ruth
Accommodations: Motels, RV parking, and camping in Ely
Finding the site: From the junction of US 6, 50, and 93 in Ely, drive northwest on US 50 for 6.8 miles to the road to the Garnet Hill Recreation Area. There is a BLM sign, but it sneaks up on you, so keep your eyes peeled. Follow the signs for about 2 miles to the collecting area. This is a very easy site to find, and there is a picnic area and ample parking at the site.

While you are at Site 47 looking for garnets, you should take a few minutes off to visit the copper pit at Ruth just across the highway.

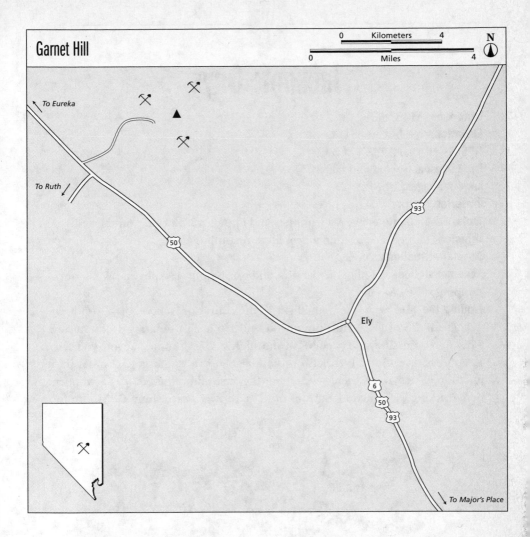

Rockhounding

As you might expect with such an accessible site, just about everyone north of the equator has been here. With patience, though, you will still find some garnets. Those with eagle eyes can still find some nice-size ones. The garnets are not of exceptional gem quality, but they do make nice specimens. A great bonus is the outstanding view of the copper pit at Ruth from the top of Garnet Hill. Don't forget the camera.

Jackpot: Onyx

Land type: Mountains
Elevation: 5,900 feet
GPS: N41 47.84' / W114 33.70'
Best season: Spring and fall
Land manager: BLM
Material: Onyx
Tools: Rock hammer (heavy hammers and chisels for working on the wall)
Vehicle: High clearance; four-wheel drive recommended
Special attractions: None
Accommodations: Motels, RV parking, and camping in Jackpot and Wells; open camping on BLM land
Finding the site: From the traffic light in the center of Jackpot, drive south on US 93 for 2.5 miles. At this point, you will see a sign pointing to Delaplain. This sign is just beyond a curve in the highway and comes up on you fast. Keep a sharp eye out. Turn left on the Delaplain road and go 3.2 miles to a junction. When I was there researching the first edition, there was a wooden post marking the junction, but this time there was a nice shiny BLM sign for

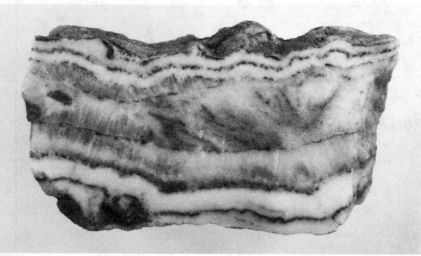

Tan and white onyx with black stripes, from the Jackpot onyx site.

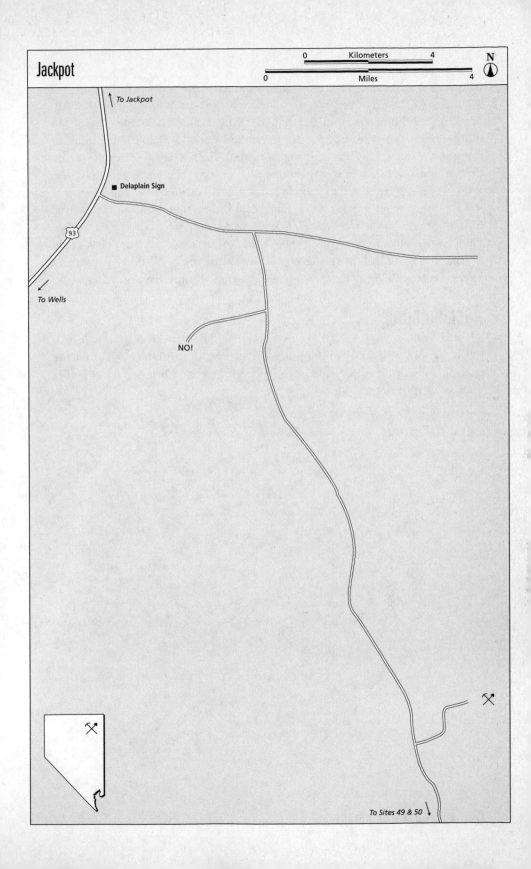

Jackpot

↑ To Jackpot

■ Delaplain Sign

93

↙ To Wells

NO!

To Sites 49 & 50 ↓

Middle Stack, Trout Creek, and Canyon Ranch. Take the left fork and drive 9.7 miles. At this point you will see a little wooden shack sitting off to the left. Look on the hillside to your left and you will see some scarring. This is the onyx mine you are heading for. An unmarked track leads about 1.5 miles to the old workings. This was a reasonably rough road when researched for the first edition, but I have to warn you that this is now a jeep track, with washouts with very steep entry and exit angles, tight turns, and unfriendly junipers that leave nice scratches in your paint. On the plus side, there is a ton of material to sort through at the top, and a lot of places to dig. There is also a really nice view of the surrounding countryside. You can relax and have lunch and try to forget that you still have to go back down that track. Would I go up there again? Probably, but my sanity has been questioned more than once.

Rockhounding

There is still some nice calcite onyx at the site. The best, of course, will have to be dug out of the side of the hill, but there are tons of small pieces for the picking all over the area. Some of the pieces fluoresce a brilliant white under long-wave ultraviolet light.

Bogwood: Opalized Wood

Land type: Hills
Elevation: 6,300 feet
GPS: N41 42.33' / W114 34.72'
Best season: Spring and fall
Land manager: BLM
Material: Opalized wood
Tools: Rock hammer
Vehicle: Any
Special attractions: None
Accommodations: Motels, RV parking, and camping in Jackpot and Wells; open camping on BLM land

Finding the site: From the turn-off to the track to the onyx mine at Site 48, continue down the road for 2.9 miles to a fork. Take the left fork for 1.1 miles to another fork. Turn right at this fork and proceed another 3.6 miles. Here a road goes right to a little hill covered with junipers. Drive about 0.2 mile into the trees and park.

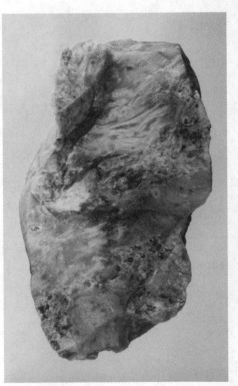

Rockhounding

This is a really nice area both for rockhounding and for camping. Even though it has been pretty well picked over, there is still quite a bit left. But it will take some roaming and maybe a little minor digging to get the best. On the west slope of the hill, I found dozens of little twig and branch sections with whitish

Opalized wood from the Bogwood site.

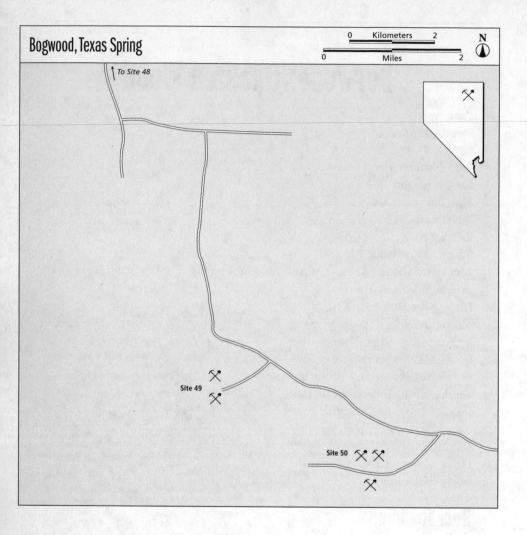

To Site 48

Site 49

Site 50

bark imprints on the outside and with opal centers. Most are only an inch or two in length, but they are really nice specimens, and some fluoresce a pretty green under shortwave ultraviolet light.

NOTE: In the first edition I mistakenly called this site Opal Spring. Opal Spring is several miles away. Oops!

Texas Spring: Petrified Wood

See map on page 128.

Land type: Hills
Elevation: 5,900 feet
GPS: N41 40.25' / W114 33.64'
Best season: Spring and fall
Land manager: BLM
Material: Wood casts, agate
Tools: Rock hammer, heavy digging tools
Vehicle: High clearance
Special attractions: None
Accommodations: Motels, RV parking, and camping in Jackpot and Wells; open camping on BLM land
Finding the site: From the turnoff to Site 49, drive south for 2.4 miles to a road going right. Take this road for about 0.7 mile, to where you will see a hill on the right. In the first edition, I wrote that "The top of this hill looks like a convention of super gophers met here." As I think about it, it looked more like a bombing range. On researching it for the second edition, however, it looks like no human has ever touched it. At first, I thought I had read my own directions wrong, but GPS confirmed that I was where I was supposed to be. When I got home, I called the BLM office in Wells and talked with a geologist who told me that evidently a club, or clubs, had met out there and had cleaned the place up. I'll bet there is still some great material out there, but it will take a lot more walking, stooping, and digging to find it. By the way, if you do dig and don't find anything, how about taking out your frustration by filling in the hole?

NOTE: The GPS coordinates are from the USGS topo for Texas Spring, which is a short way off the roads. It is given just to get you to the general area.

Rockhounding

Even though the main site has been filled in, I keep hearing reports of limb casts still being found in the Texas Spring area. It is a little remote, but there is a nice dry camping area right off the road, so if you can, spend some time here and do some roaming, I'll bet there is one of those big pink limb casts just waiting for you to discover it.

Contact: Malachite, Chrysocolla

Land type: Hills
Elevation: 5,400 feet
GPS: N41 45.06' / W114 45.84' (at the road gate)
Best season: Spring through fall
Land manager: BLM
Material: Malachite, chrysocolla
Tools: Rock hammer
Vehicle: High clearance
Special attractions: None
Accommodations: Motels, RV parking, and camping in Jackpot and Wells; open camping on BLM land
Finding the site: From the tiny town of Contact, drive south on US 93 for 1.6 miles to a road going left. If the odometers don't match, just be sure you are on the south side of the bridge over Salmon Falls Creek. There is a road on the north side at the approximate mileage, but it dead-ends at the creek. At the

Green malachite on quartz, from Contact.

The mineral samples at Contact are in the ridges just above the old structure in the center of this photo.

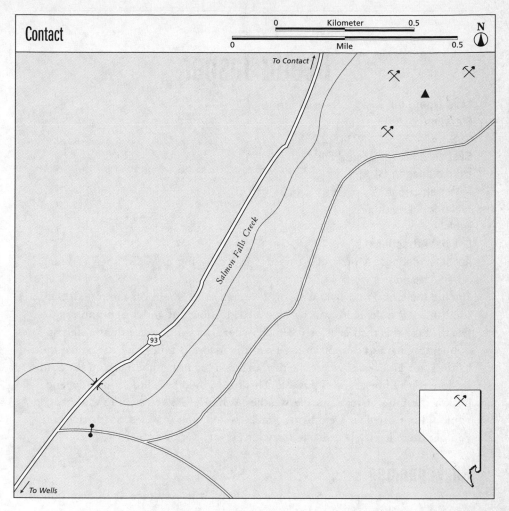

correct road there is a BLM sign with the mileage to Middlestack Mountain and Meadow Creek. Go through the gate, turn left, and follow the road as it turns back north. At a little over 1 mile, you will see the old mine and buildings on your left. Park by the abandoned buildings.

NOTE: The GPS coordinates are given for the gate at the highway turnoff, since this is the most easily missed point.

Rockhounding

There is a lot of malachite and chrysocolla on the dumps here, but it is too thin to be of lapidary use. The colors are bright and nice, though, and since it is so close to the highway, it is worth the trip.

Deeth: Jasper

Land type: Hills
Elevation: 6,200 feet
GPS: N41 22.53' / W115 21.58'
Best season: Spring and fall
Land manager: BLM
Material: Jasper
Tools: Rock hammer
Vehicle: Any
Special attractions: None
Accommodations: Motels, RV parking, and camping at Wells; open camping on BLM land
Finding the site: From I-80 west of Wells, take the Deeth off-ramp (exit 333) south for 0.8 mile. Here you will see a road going left and a sign pointing to Deeth. Take this road east for 0.8 mile, where a road goes north at a sign announcing Charleston in 50 miles. Take this road 8.6 miles to a fork. Take the left fork for 17.1 miles, where the road makes a big horseshoe. Park off the road as close to the horseshoe as possible. This road could be a little rough depending on the time of year and the weather. When I was researching the second edition, long stretches were being graded, oiled, and graveled, so by the time you get there it may be suitable for your Ferrari. Or not.

Rockhounding

There is a lot of jasper out here, and some of it is very nice. It is spread out over a big area, though. I had the best luck on the west side of the road near the top of the horseshoe.

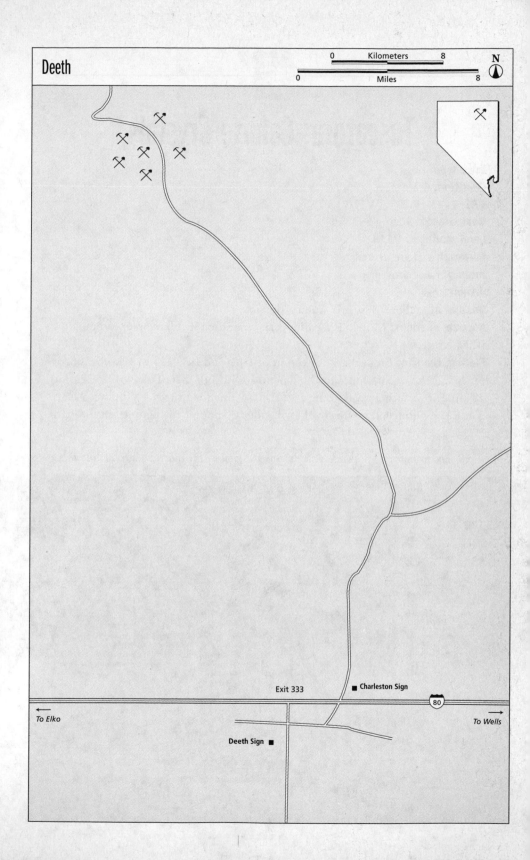

Deeth

Kilometers
0 8

Miles
0 8

N

Exit 333   ■ Charleston Sign

80

← To Elko

To Wells →

Deeth Sign ■

Tuscarora: Calcite Crystals

Land type: Hills
Elevation: 6,400 feet
GPS: N41 19.29' / W116 13.78'
Best season: Spring and fall
Land manager: BLM
Material: Calcite crystals
Tools: Rock hammer
Vehicle: Any
Special attractions: Historic mining district
Accommodations: Motels, RV parking, and camping in Elko; open camping on BLM land
Finding the site: From the intersection of I-80 and NV 225 in Elko, go north on NV 225 for 26.1 miles to the junction with NV 226. Follow NV 226 for 18 miles to another road going left. Follow this road for 5.4 miles to a road going right. Proceed up this road for 1 mile to another road going left through

From the old smokestack, you have a 360-degree view of the collecting area at Tuscarora.

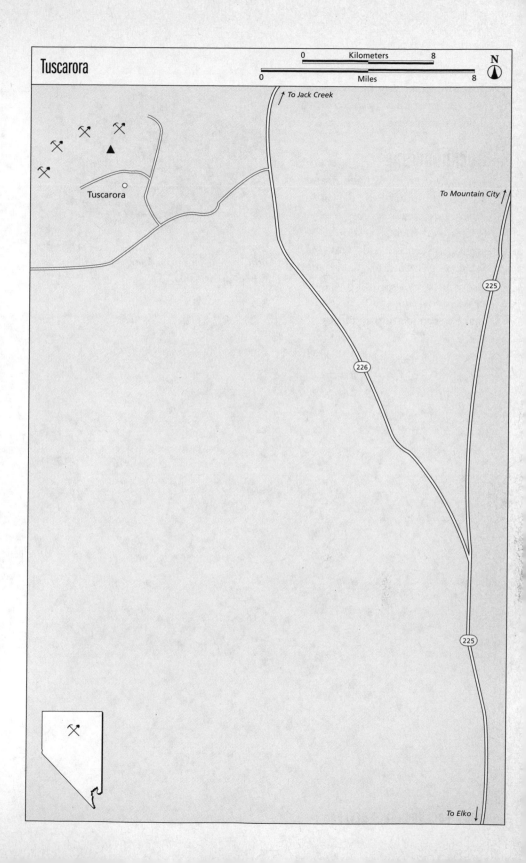

Tuscarora

0 Kilometers 8

0 Miles 8

N

To Jack Creek

To Mountain City

225

226

225

Tuscarora

To Elko

Tuscarora. Take any of the roads out of town that head for the huge tailings piles.

Rockhounding

Hunt all over these tailings and all of the others in the area. There are roads going everywhere out here, so don't be afraid to venture out and see what you can find. There are some nice "plates" with calcite crystals covering the faces. These make very nice display pieces.

Calcite crystals on brown matrix, from tailings piles at Tuscarora.

Ferdelford Canyon: Fossils

Land type: Hills
Elevation: 5,354 feet
GPS: N40 33.25' / W116 05.34'
Best season: Spring and fall
Land manager: BLM
Material: Marine fossil shells, crinoids, calcite

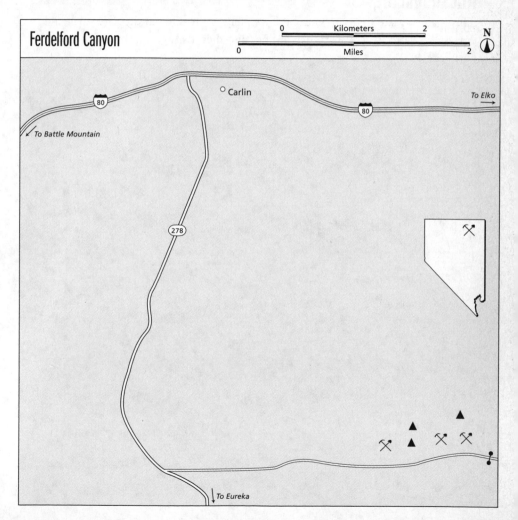

Tools: Rock hammer
Vehicle: Any
Special attractions: None
Accommodations: Motels, RV parking, and camping in Carlin
Finding the site: From the junction of I-80 and NV 278 in Carlin, drive south on NV 278 for 14.4 miles to a dirt road on the left. Follow this road for about 2.5 miles to the hills on the left. If you come to a gate, you went a bit too far. Go back a hundred yards or so, park, and hunt in the hills on the north side of the road.

Rockhounding

This is an easy site to get to and there are plenty of fossils, but they are small and you will have to keep a sharp eye out because they will try and hide from you.

Black Shale Hill: Fossils

Land type: Hills
Elevation: 5,598 feet
GPS: N40 51.94' / W115 51.9'
Best season: Spring through fall
Land manager: BLM
Material: Marine fossils
Tools: Rock hammer
Vehicle: Any
Special attractions: None
Accommodations: Motels, RV parking, and camping in Elko; open camping on BLM land
Finding the site: From the junction of I-80 and NV 225 in Elko, drive northwest on NV 225 for 4 miles to a gravel road on the right. Turn off on this road, park, and hunt on the black shale hill.

Small marine fossils abound at Black Shale Hill.

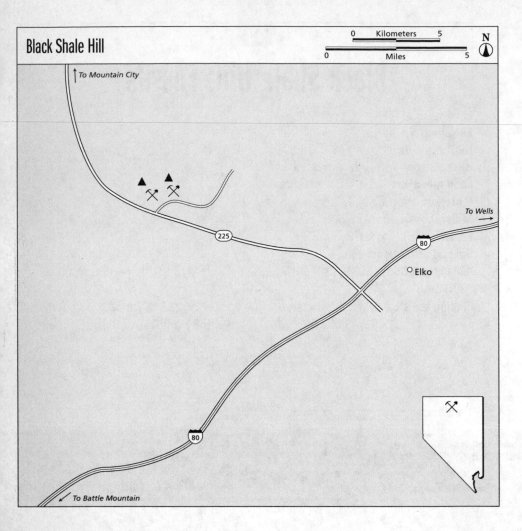

0 Kilometers 5

0 Miles 5

N

↑ To Mountain City

225

To Wells →

80

○ Elko

80

← To Battle Mountain

Rockhounding

This is a nice site for anyone, but the kids should love it for all of the nice little fossils. Mom and dad will love it because it is only 4 miles from the interstate, right next to a paved highway, and offers a break from long miles of driving.

The road continues past the first hill for a short distance to some more black hills, but I did not find these as productive. You may discover that I should have looked more closely.

Copper Basin: Leaf Fossils

Land type: Mountains
Elevation: 7,400 feet
GPS: N41 44.77' / W115 28.49'
Best season: Spring through fall
Land manager: Humboldt National Forest
Material: Leaf fossils
Tools: Rock hammer, shale splitting tools
Vehicle: Any
Special attractions: Historic town of Jarbidge
Accommodations: Motels, RV parking, and camping in Elko; open camping on BLM land
Finding the site: From the intersection of I-80 and NV 225 in Elko, go north on NV 225 for 53.4 miles to a road heading east. The road is well marked with a sign indicating that it is the way to Jarbidge. Take this road east for 21 miles to a fork. Take the left fork for 6.4 miles to another fork. Take the road to the

The tiny white spot in the center of this picture is the Copper Basin shale where leaf fossils are found.

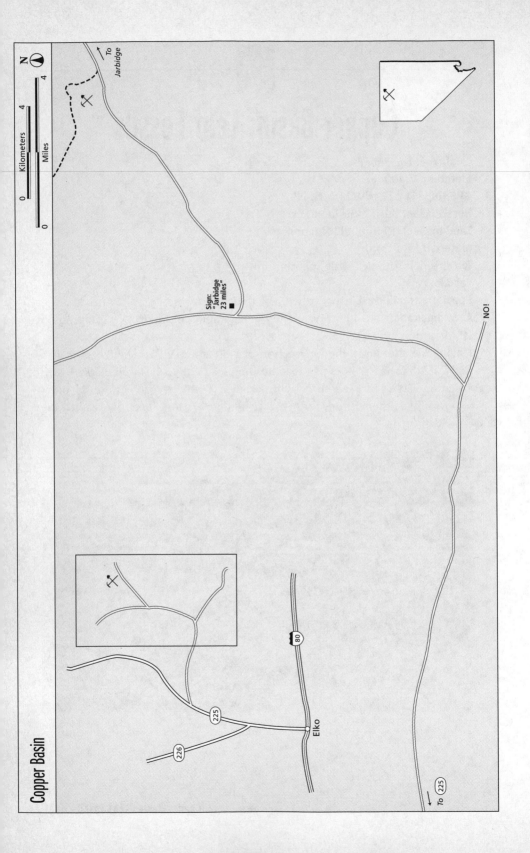

Copper Basin

N

Kilometers
0   4
Miles
0   4

To
Jarbidge

Sign:
"Jarbidge
23 miles"

225

226

Elko

80

To 225

101

right and travel 6.9 miles where you will see a rough track going to the left. At this point, you will be high above the canyon floor. Pull onto the road, which is very steep and extremely rough. That's the bad news. The good news is that it is only 0.5 mile to the site. If you have four-wheel drive you can drive to the site. If you don't, you will have to walk. I've done both, and it is a toss-up. It is a steep hike, but not too bad. On the other hand, it is rocky and miserable on the tires. You choose.

Fossil leaf imprint from Copper Basin.

No matter which means you choose, look off to the left and downhill before you start. About halfway to the canyon floor and just to the left of the road you are on, you will see a large grayish white patch. That's what you are heading for. It is a little hard to see from the road, so keep the location in mind.

Rockhounding

When you arrive, you will see where others have been industrious. Look around to see what they have been digging and you will get an idea of what to look for. There are lots of partial leaves in the tailings, but you will have to do some digging and shale splitting to find whole ones. There is a lot of hillside to explore here, so don't be afraid to seek out your own diggings. Who knows, you may find a new spot with some great whole leaves.

This is also a very beautiful and peaceful spot, so take along a picnic lunch and do a little communing with nature (and a ham-and-cheese sandwich).

Daisy Creek: Petrified Wood

Land type: Low mountains
Elevation: 5,500 feet
GPS: N40 15.40' / W117 20.77'
Best season: Spring and fall
Land manager: BLM
Material: Petrified wood, wonderstone
Tools: Rock hammer, heavy digging tools
Vehicle: High clearance
Special attractions: None
Accommodations: Motels, RV parking, and camping in the Battle Mountain area; open camping on BLM land
Finding the site: From the intersection of NV 305 and I-80 in Battle Mountain, drive south on NV 305 for 11.3 miles to a road going right. This road is marked for Copper Canyon and Buffalo Valley. Follow this road, keeping left at each of the next two forks. At 20.7 miles you will come to a road going left. Turn onto this road and head toward the mountains.

This is very empty country out here, and landmarks are few. You will know that you are on the right road if you see a large wire corral on the right at about 1.5 miles from the left-hand turn. From the corral the road winds up through a narrow canyon. Daisy Creek is in the gorge to the right.

At 4.7 miles from the turnoff, you will come out of the canyon into a little meadow. On the left, you will see the site, some big diggings where heavy machinery has been working.

Beautiful dendritic patterns from Daisy Creek.

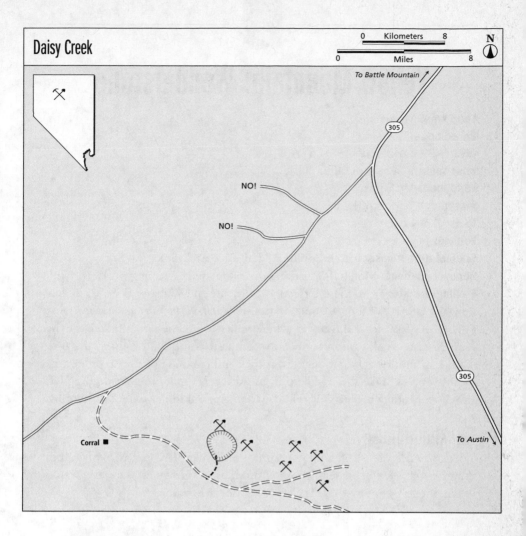

Daisy Creek

0 Kilometers 8
0 Miles 8

N

To Battle Mountain

305

NO!

NO!

305

Corral

To Austin

Rockhounding

This is another very old and very large collecting area, and a lot of material has been taken out. I contemplated not including it in this second edition, because I didn't find much this time, but it has been so productive over the years that I decided to leave it in. Be sure to wander away from the roads and the obvious diggings, and when you find some small pieces, do a little digging. I can't promise that you will find anything, but I just have a feeling. Of course, if you don't find anything, I'm sure you will have some choice thoughts about my decision.

Yellow Mountain: Wonderstone

Land type: Mountains
Elevation: 4,249 feet
GPS: N39 24.50' / W118 34.57'
Best season: Spring through fall
Land manager: BLM
Material: Wonderstone
Tools: Rock hammer
Vehicle: High clearance
Special attractions: Grimes Point/Hidden Cave Archaeological Site
Accommodations: Motels, RV parking in Fallon; open camping on BLM land
Finding the site: From the intersection of Maine and Williams (US 50) in Fallon, take US 50 east for 10.1 miles to the well-marked turnoff to Grimes Point. Follow this road for 1.2 miles to where you will see the parking area for the Hidden Cave Trail. Continue on for 0.8 mile to a fork. Go right at the fork for 0.1 to another fork. Go left at this fork and continue on for 0.3 mile to a three-way fork. Take the middle tine and drive 1.5 miles to a road going left to Yellow Mountain. Head for Yellow Mountain, and in 0.4 mile start hunting.

Rockhounding

There has been a lot of mining on the north side of Yellow Mountain, but there is still a lot of material on and around the mountain. Don't take too much, though, because there is a lot to come farther along.

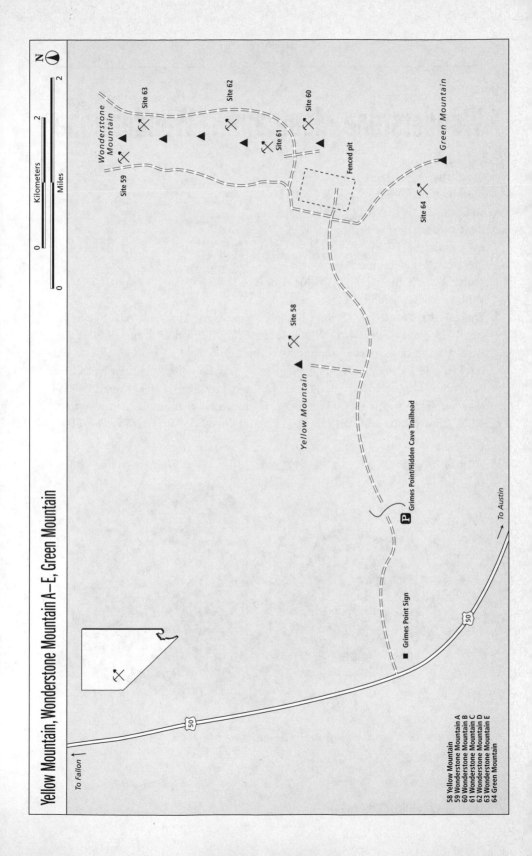

Yellow Mountain, Wonderstone Mountain A–E, Green Mountain

Kilometers
0   2

Miles
0   2

N

Wonderstone Mountain

Site 59
Site 63
Site 62
Site 61
Site 60
Site 64

Fenced pit

Green Mountain

Yellow Mountain

Site 58

Grimes Point/Hidden Cave Trailhead

Grimes Point Sign

To Fallon

To Austin

50
50

58 Yellow Mountain
59 Wonderstone Mountain A
60 Wonderstone Mountain B
61 Wonderstone Mountain C
62 Wonderstone Mountain D
63 Wonderstone Mountain E
64 Green Mountain

Wonderstone Mountain A: Wonderstone

See map on page 147.

Land type: Mountains

Elevation: 4,100 feet

GPS: N39 24.71' / W118 33.06'

Best season: Spring through fall

Land manager: BLM

Material: Wonderstone

Tools: Rock hammer, heavy hammer, and chisels

Vehicle: High clearance

Special attractions: The Grimes Point–Hidden Cave Archaeological Site is located 1.5 miles down Grimes Point Road from the turnoff from US 50. From here it is possible to take a short hike through a field of petroglyph-covered boulders, and a slightly longer, guided hike to a cave that was used by Native Americans between 3,400 and 4,000 years ago. The area was first visited by Native Americans nearly 8,000 years ago. For information about the tours, contact: BLM Office, 5665 Morgan Hill Rd., Carson City, NV 89701; (775) 885-6000;

Wonderstone in red and white from the Wonderstone Mountain A site.

ccfoweb@blm.gov or Churchill County Museum, 1050 South Maine St., Fallon, NV 89406; (775) 423-3677; director@ccmuseum.org

Accommodations: Motels, RV parking, and camping in the Fallon area; open camping on BLM land

Finding the site: From the intersection of Maine and Williams (US 50) in Fallon, take US 50 east for 10.1 miles to the Grimes Point turnoff. Take this road to the left. At 1.2 miles, you will see Hidden Cave parking area. Continue on for another 0.8 mile to a fork. Keep right. Go 0.1 mile to another fork. Keep left. At 0.3 mile farther, there is a three-way fork. Take the middle tine. At 1.5 miles, you will see the road to Yellow Mountain on the left. Keep straight ahead. At 1.2 miles the road makes a 90-degree turn to the left at a fence around a large pit. Follow the road along the fence as it turns right around the pit and climbs the hill. At about 0.4 mile a road goes left into the valley. Take this road for 0.7 mile as it parallels Wonderstone Mountain on the right. Here a dirt track goes 0.3 mile toward the mountain. You will see a cut lined with wonderstone running into the mountain. Park anywhere off the road and start picking up wonderstone.

Rockhounding

This is still another old site, but the mountain seems to be made of wonderstone, so there is no shortage of material. I believe that this side of the mountain is the original site, and while the material here is just as nice as that on the other side, it is not quite as plentiful. Search all along the mountain and poke into all of the nooks and crannies.

Red, white, tan, and black wonderstone from the Wonderstone Mountain A site.

Wonderstone Mountain B: Wonderstone

See map on page 147.

Land type: Mountains
Elevation: 4,340 feet
GPS: N39 24.12' / W118 33.22'
Best season: Spring through fall
Land manager: BLM
Material: Wonderstone
Tools: Rock hammer
Vehicle: High clearance
Special attractions: Grimes Point–Hidden Cave Archaeological Site
Accommodations: Motels, RV parking, and camping in the Fallon area; open camping on BLM land.
Finding the site: From Site 59, drive back to the road that came up from the pit. Take the first road to the left and go 0.2 mile to a track crossing the one you are on. Go right for about 0.1 mile, park, and hunt on both sides of the track.

Rockhounding

There is some very nice material at this end of the mountain, but then again the whole mountain is wonderstone. You will just have to decide which you think is best.

Wonderstone Mountain C: Wonderstone

See map on page 147.
Land type: Mountains
Elevation: 4,386 feet
GPS: N39 24.31' / W118 33.05'
Best season: Spring through fall
Land manager: BLM
Material: Wonderstone
Tools: Rock hammer
Vehicle: High clearance
Special attractions: Grimes Point–Hidden Cave Archaeological Site
Accommodations: Motels, RV parking, and camping in the Fallon area; open camping on BLM land
Finding the site: From Site 60, drive back to the crossroad. Keep straight ahead for about 0.1 mile. Park and hunt on both sides of the road and up the hill.

Rockhounding

Here you will find still more wonderstone and maybe a rare piece of agate.

Wonderstone Mountain D: Wonderstone

See map on page 147.

Land type: Mountains
Elevation: 4,370 feet
GPS: N39 24.31' / W118 32.90'
Best season: Spring through fall
Land manager: BLM
Material: Wonderstone
Tools: Rock hammer
Vehicle: High clearance
Special attractions: Grimes Point–Hidden Cave Archaeological Site
Accommodations: Motels, RV parking, and camping in the Fallon area; open camping on BLM land
Finding the site: From Site 61, return to the crossroad and go left. Follow the road as it curves left and heads north up the east side of the mountain. At 0.2 mile from the crossroad, pull off anywhere along the road and hunt up the slopes.

Rockhounding

This is the area where I found the nicest material when researching the first edition. There is still a mountain (no pun intended) of material here. Look for the hardest stuff. Some of it will take a nice polish.

Wonderstone Mountain E: Wonderstone

See map on page 147.
Land type: Mountains
Elevation: 4,399 feet
GPS: N39 24.36' / W118 32.83'
Best season: Spring through fall
Land manager: BLM
Material: Wonderstone
Tools: Rock hammer
Vehicle: High clearance
Special attractions: Grimes Point–Hidden Cave Archaeological Site
Accommodations: Motels, RV parking, and camping in the Fallon area; open camping on BLM land
Finding the site: From Site 62, drive about 0.1 mile, park and hunt on the mountainside.

Rockhounding

The material here is more of the same, and there is a lot of it. You should have bags, boxes, and your pockets full by now, so finish up and head over to Green Mountain.

Green Mountain: Wonderstone, Green Rhyolite

See map on page 147.
Land type: Mountains
Elevation: 4,219 feet
GPS: N39 23.54' / W118 33.40'
Best season: Spring through fall
Land manager: BLM
Material: Wonderstone, green rhyolite
Tools: Rock hammer
Vehicle: High clearance
Special attractions: Grimes Point–Hidden Cave Archaeological Site
Accommodations: Motels, RV parking, and camping in the Fallon area; open camping on BLM land
Finding the site: From the intersection of Maine and Williams (US 50) in Fallon, take US 50 east for 10.1 miles to the Grimes Point turnoff. Take this road to the left. At 1.2 miles, you will see Hidden Cave trailhead parking area. Continue for another 0.8 mile to a fork. Keep right. Go 0.1 mile to another fork. Keep left. At 0.3 mile farther, there is a three-way fork. Take the middle tine. At 1.5 miles, you will see the road to Yellow Mountain on the left. Keep straight ahead.

At 1.2 miles there is a fence enclosing a large pit. Go right around the pit and follow the road toward the very obvious green mountain standing all by itself in the middle of the desert. There are lots of roads out here, but just keep heading for the mountain. If you make a wrong road choice, just go back and try another. There are many roads, tracks, and jeep trails in the Wonderstone Mountain area. If you follow the mileages carefully, you will have no trouble. Of course, GPS is a major plus in areas like this.

Rockhounding

The washes, the flanks of the mountain, and the flat desert all around here are good hunting areas. You will find lots of pieces of wonderstone like that from Wonderstone Mountain, but the most interesting material is the green rock.

Green Mountain is impossible to miss as it pokes up from the center of an otherwise flat desert.

The whole mountain is made of this stuff. I believe it is rhyolite, but some of it looks almost like jade, and some of it looks like jasper. Most of it, however, looks like green sidewalk. Take home some of the good-looking stuff and see what you can make with it. There have been numerous reports of nice agate on the lower flanks of the mountain, too. Take some time and do some stooping. It's great exercise, and you might hit the mother lode.

Bench Creek: Plant Fossils, Opal

Land type: Hills
Elevation: 4,900 feet
GPS: N39 18.56' / W117 58.81'
Best season: Spring through fall
Land manager: BLM
Material: Plant fossils, opal
Tools: Rock hammer, shale splitting tools
Vehicle: High clearance/four-wheel drive
Special attractions: None
Accommodations: Motels, RV parking, and camping in the Fallon area; open camping on BLM land
Finding the site: From the junction of US 50 and NV 361 about 50 miles east of Fallon, go east on US 50 for 2 miles. Here a faint road goes left. It is hard to see, but it is marked with a sign for Bench Creek Ranch. If you miss it, turn around at the little pullout by a big tree just past the indicated mileage. The tree is hung with hundreds of shoes. Yes, I said shoes. I have no idea what this signifies, but you probably should take a picture just in case anyone doubts your story.

When you find the road, you will see that it drops down from the highway, crosses a little creek, and goes around the end of the mountain. At 0.5 mile from the highway, another track goes right. Follow this for 1.0 mile and park off the road. When researching the first edition, I hiked from this point, but for the second edition it was possible to drive down into the valley and around from hill to hill. Driving saves a little time and energy, but more can be seen by walking.

No matter which method you choose, head generally south toward US 50. In 0.2 mile or so, you will come to a little ridge. At the east end of the ridge, there are a lot of interesting common opal chips. If you continue on to the east, you will come to a large white hill. If you don't see it, keep going. You will know when you arrive because the hill is covered with diggings, and it is the last hill before a long stretch of flat desert.

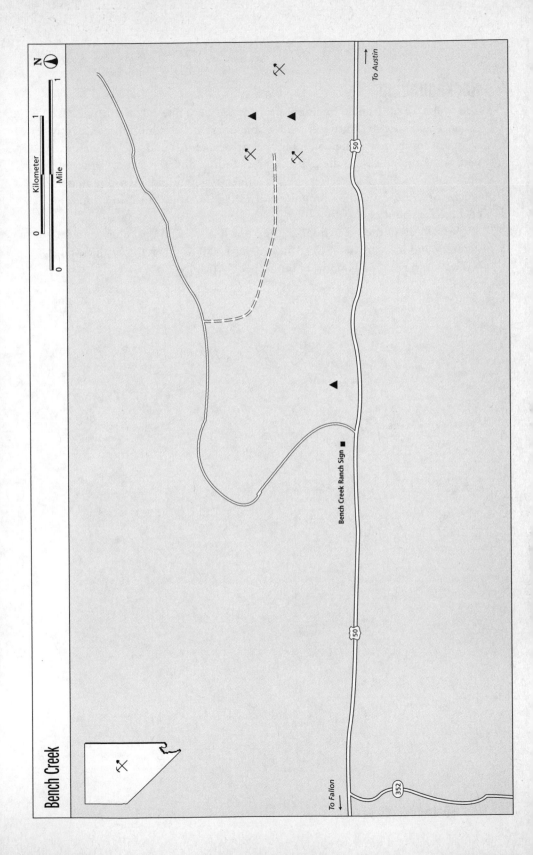

Bench Creek

To Austin

To Fallon

Bench Creek Ranch Sign ■

50

50

352

N

Kilometer
0   1

Mile
0   1

Rockhounding

You will have no trouble finding leaf fossils on the white hill, but it will take patience and a lot of splitting to find whole ones. At one time, there evidently were leaf fossils in a white common opal or opalite. I found a few little chips with some tiny fossils on them. If you were to find a whole leaf on a piece of opal, you would have a real treasure. Of course, if you found a ten-pound gold nugget or a pickup-load of turquoise you would be happy too. And I think the chances are about equal.

Virtually all of the valley floor and the low hills contain opal chips, and fossils are found in many spots. Keep an eye out for spots where others have dug. It always surprises me how many things people overlook.

Buffalo Canyon A: Plant Fossils

Land type: Hills
Elevation: 5,900 feet
GPS: N39 12.37' / W117 49.01'
Best season: Spring and fall
Land manager: BLM
Material: Plant fossils
Tools: Small digging tools, splitting tools
Vehicle: High clearance
Special attractions: None
Accommodations: Motels, RV parking, and camping in the Fallon area; open camping on BLM land
Finding the site: From the junction of US 50 and NV 722, located a little over 50 miles east of Fallon, take NV 722 southeast for 7.6 miles to a road going

Plant fossils are abundant on the flanks of the hill in Buffalo Canyon. They are very fragile though, so handle with care.

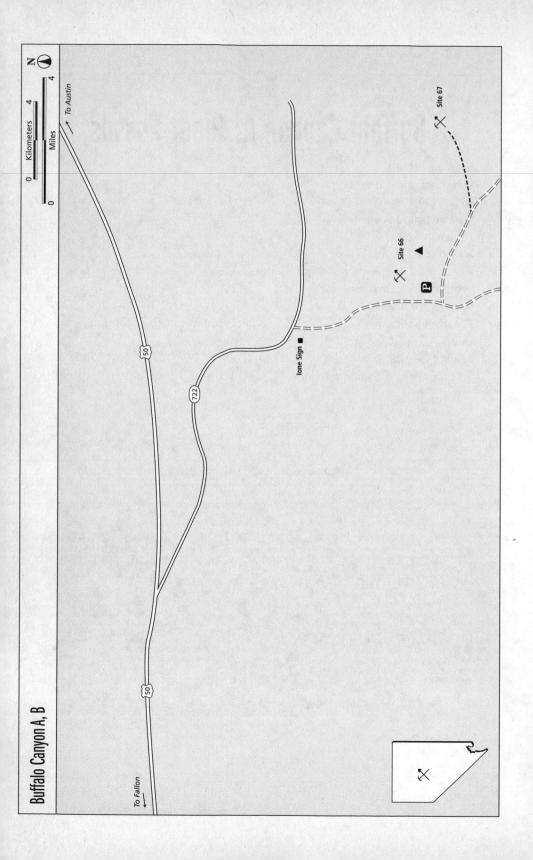

Buffalo Canyon A, B

N

Kilometers
0   4

Miles
0   4

To Austin

To Fallon

50

50

722

Ione Sign

Site 66

P

Site 67

right. The road will be marked to Ione and Buffalo Canyon. Follow this road for 5 miles to a road going left. At just 0.1 there is a parking spot. Search on the hillside and on the flats.

Rockhounding

You can find plenty of fossils in the rubble that others have left, but, as always, the best will be found by digging and splitting. These specimens are in a soft matrix, so be sure to have some means of protecting them. All of the agate, opal, selenite, and quartz is small and scattered, but in a short time you should be able to gather a respectable little pile.

A leaf imprint from Buffalo Canyon A, Site 66. The leaf is brown on white shale.

Buffalo Canyon B: Common Opal, Opalite

See map on page 160.
Land type: Hills, mine
Elevation: 6,100 feet
Best season: Spring through fall
GPS: N39 11.92' / 117 47.45'
Land manager: BLM
Material: Common opal, opalite
Tools: Rock hammer
Vehicle: High clearance
Special attractions: None

This road leads to the old diatomite mine at Site 67. Opal can be found in the "fossil flour" around the cedars.

Accommodations: Motels, RV parking, and camping in the Fallon area; open camping on BLM land

Finding the site: From the junction of US 50 and NV 722, located a little over 50 miles east of Fallon, take NV 722 southeast for 7.6 miles to a road going right. The road will be marked to Ione and Buffalo Canyon. Follow this road for 5 miles to a road going left. At just 0.1 mile is the parking spot for Site 66. Continue past the parking spot and keep left for 0.7 mile to a fork. Go left and proceed another 0.9 mile. Here you will see some mine workings on the left. Park off the road.

Rockhounding

If the mine is working, don't go on the property. There is plenty of material all over the area below the mine, so there is really no reason to go up there anyway. There are some fairly large pieces of common opal and opalite here, and they come in a variety of colors and patterns. This is not precious opal by any means, but there are pieces that will make up into nice cabochons.

Common opal from Buffalo Canyon B, Site 67.

Kaiser Mine Road: Jasper, Agate

Land type: Hills
Elevation: 5,583 feet
GPS: N39 02.71' / W118 05.04'
Best season: Spring and fall
Land manager: BLM
Material: Agate, jasper
Tools: Rock hammer
Vehicle: Any
Special attractions: Berlin-Ichthyosaur State Park
Accommodations: Camping at Berlin-Ichthyosaur State Park near Gabbs; open camping on BLM land; the nearest motels are in Hawthorne and Fallon
Finding the site: From Gabbs drive north on NV 361 for about 13 miles to the well-marked Nye County/Mineral County line. Check your odometer here and drive 0.2 mile to a dirt road on your left. Drive west on the dirt road for 3 miles and park along the road. From this point, hunt in the low hills on both sides of the road for a mile or two to the west.

Rockhounding

There is a lot of agate and jasper on these hills, and much of it is of good quality. It is scattered, however, and you will have to do some walking to find the best. It is a pretty spot, though, and if you chose a nice spring or fall day it will be an enjoyable hunt.

This beautiful red, yellow, and blue jasper chunk is from Kaiser Mine Road.

Kaiser Mine Road, Kaiser Mine, North of Gabbs A, B

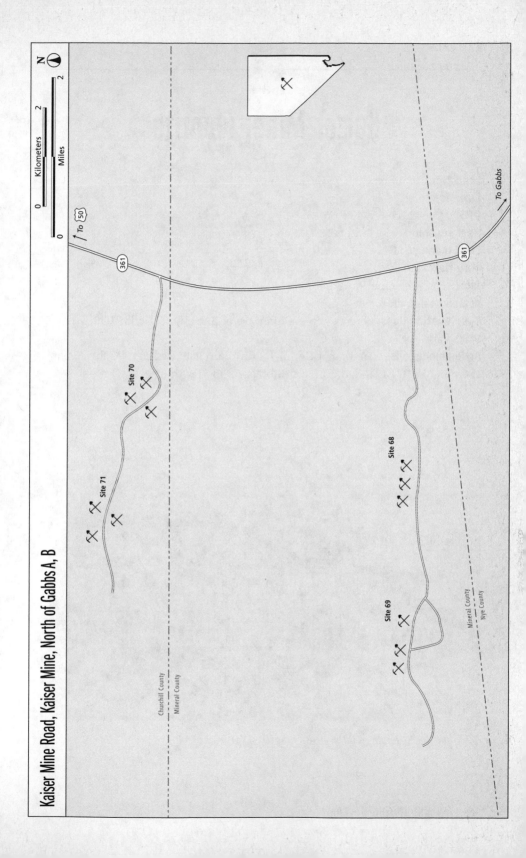

Kaiser Mine: Fluorite

See map on page 165.

Land type: Mountains

Elevation: 6,000 feet

GPS: N39 02.83' / W118 06.13'

Best season: Spring and fall

Land manager: BLM

Material: Fluorite

Tools: Rock hammer

Vehicle: High clearance

Special attractions: Ghost town buildings beyond the mine; Berlin-Ichthyosaur State Park

Accommodations: Camping at Berlin-Ichthyosaur State Park near Gabbs; open camping on BLM land; the nearest motels are in Hawthorne and Fallon

This old shack stands guard over the fluorite at the Kaiser Mine.

Finding the site: From Site 68, drive 1 mile to the mine. Park anywhere and wander around. If you have a high-clearance vehicle or four-wheel drive, you can drive farther up the hill and over to the old ghost buildings on the back slope of the mountain.

Rockhounding

There is a lot of nice fluorite on the dumps here, and at least one really nice seam just off the road by the old machinery. The colors range from clear through smoky, and from pale blue to near amethyst. Most of it fluoresces a deep brilliant purple under long-wave ultraviolet light.

The road through the abandoned buildings goes a long way out across the valley. I don't know where it ends, but if you are the inquisitive type and have the time, give it a try.

North of Gabbs A: Jasper

See map on page 165.

Land type: Rolling hills
Elevation: 5,450 feet
GPS: N39 05.30' / W118 04.13'
Best season: Spring through fall
Land manager: BLM
Material: Jasper
Tools: Rock hammer
Vehicle: Any
Special attractions: Berlin-Ichthyosaur State Park
Accommodations: Camping at Berlin-Ichthyosaur State Park; open camping on BLM land; the closest motels are in Hawthorne and Fallon
Finding the site: From the turnoff for Site 68 north of the Mineral County/ Nye County line, continue north on NV 361 for 3.0 miles to the well-marked Mineral County/Churchill County line. Check your odometer at the county line and drive 0.3 mile to a dirt road on your left. Drive west on this road for 1.5 miles and park off the road. Hunt on both sides of the road.

Rockhounding

There are lots of small pieces of jasper scattered over a wide area. Many will yield 30 x 40 mm cabs, and some are fist size.

North of Gabbs B: Jasper, Petrified Wood

See map on page 165.
Land type: Rolling hills
Elevation: 5,501 feet
GPS: N39 05.91' / W118 05.69'
Best season: Spring through fall
Land manager: BLM
Material: Jasper, petrified wood
Tools: Rock hammer
Vehicle: Any
Special attractions: Berlin-Ichthyosaur State Park
Accommodations: Camping at Berlin-Ichthyosaur State Park; open camping on BLM land; the closest motels are in Hawthorne and Fallon
Finding the site: From Site 70, continue west on the dirt road for another 1.5 miles. Park off the road.

Rockhounding

Hunt on both sides of the road for jasper and silicified wood. As at Site 70, the pieces are small and scattered, but a little walking and stooping will make the trip worthwhile.

Kernick Mine: Selenite

Land type: Hills
Elevation: 5,200 feet
GPS: N38 19.66' / W118 08.14'
Best season: Spring and fall
Land manager: BLM
Material: Selenite
Tools: Rock hammer
Vehicle: Any
Special attractions: None
Accommodations: Motels in Hawthorne; public RV parking and camping at Walker Lake and Berlin-Ichthyosaur State Park near Gabbs; open camping on BLM land
Finding the site: From the fire department building on US 95 in Mina, drive south on the highway for 3.7 miles to a road going right. Turn onto the road and take the right fork that swings north. Follow this road for 2.1 miles to the mine.

Rockhounding

When I was there, it appeared that the mine was totally abandoned. There were no signs of activity, no machinery, no postings, and no closed or locked gates. There was still quite a bit of selenite on the piles near the road outside the mine property. Some of the chunks were nearly a foot across. If you don't want such chunks, there are lots of little pieces, too. If you have a high-clearance vehicle, you might also want to drive up the right fork near the mine gate and see what you can find. I found a little jasper, but I didn't spend much time there.

The mine itself is just a huge open pit operation. There were also a lot of chips and small pieces in the walls and on the rubble in the mine. A little work could probably turn up some big pieces, too.

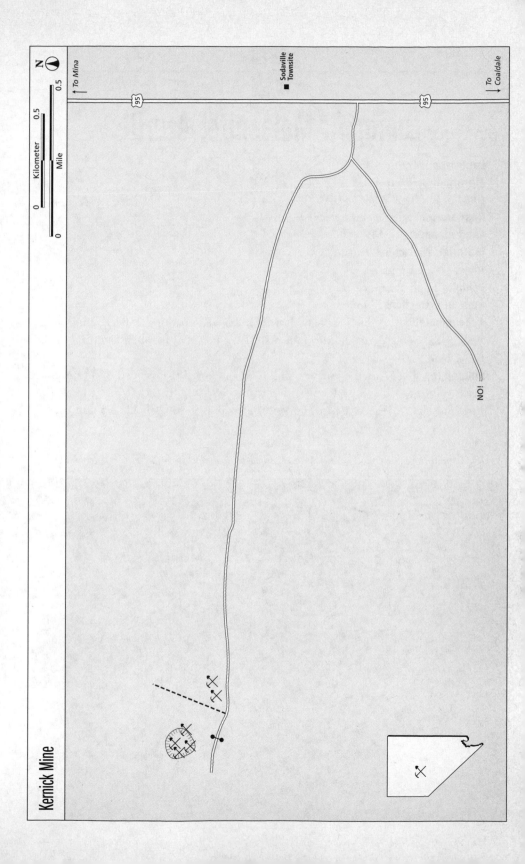

Kernick Mine

Luning A: Malachite, Azurite

Land type: Mountains
Elevation: 4,575 feet
GPS: N38 30.12' / W118 07.61'
Best season: Spring through fall
Land manager: BLM
Material: Malachite, azurite
Tools: Rock hammer
Vehicle: High clearance
Special attractions: None
Accommodations: Motels in Hawthorne; public RV parking and camping at Walker Lake and Berlin-Ichthyosaur State Park near Gabbs; open camping on BLM land
Finding the site: From the junction of US 95 and NV 361 just north of Luning, drive southeast on US 95 for 0.7 mile to the rest stop. Turn left into the rest stop and right at the dirt road. Follow the road as it parallels US 95 and the

This small mound at the Luning A site is filled with malachite and azurite specimens.

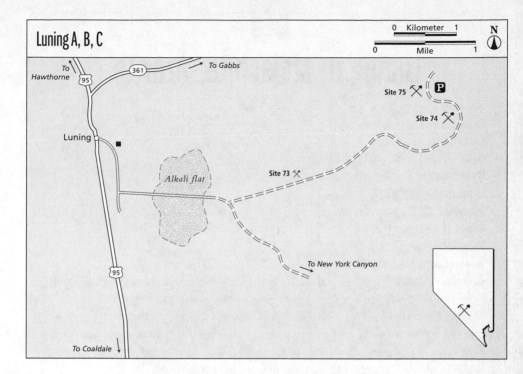

0 Kilometer 1

0 Mile 1

N

To Hawthorne — 95

361 — To Gabbs

Site 75

P

Site 74

Luning

Alkali flat

Site 73

To New York Canyon

95

To Coaldale

alkali lake on the left. At 0.7 mile from the rest stop, a road goes left across the dry lake. Follow this road across the lake. As you leave the lake, you will come to a fork. Take the left fork for 2.3 miles to an old pile of tailings on the left.

Rockhounding

This small pile is filled with nice samples of both malachite and azurite on a white or tan matrix. It is mostly stain and very thin pieces good for display, but not for lapidary. Once in a while, though, there will be a piece solid enough and of a size that it would be suitable for small cabs in earrings, etc.

Luning B: Malachite, Azurite

See map on page 173.

Land type: Mountains
Elevation: 5,298 feet
GPS: N38 30.48' / W118 06.04'
Best season: Spring through fall
Land manager: BLM
Material: Malachite, azurite
Tools: Rock hammer
Vehicle: High clearance
Special attractions: None
Accommodations: Motels in Hawthorne; public RV parking and camping at Walker Lake and Berlin-Ichthyosaur State Park near Gabbs; open camping on BLM land
Finding the site: From Site 73 off US 95 outside Luning, continue up the canyon for 1.8 miles to an old mine on the right. Pull over as far as possible and park. If it is not possible to park because of the berm turned up by a grader, keep on about 0.1 mile and park on the big flat to the left.

Rockhounding

There is a lot of material to check out at this site. Some really nice specimens of malachite and azurite on matrix can be found.

You can fill your rock bag with nice malachite and azurite samples from the old mine at the Luning B site.

Luning C: Malachite, Azurite

See map on page 173.
Land type: Mountains
Elevation: 5,377 feet
GPS: N38 30.58' / W118 05.97'
Best season: Spring through fall
Land manager: BLM
Material: Malachite, azurite
Tools: Rock hammer
Vehicle: High clearance
Special attractions: None
Accommodations: Motels in Hawthorne; public RV parking and camping at Walker Lake and Berlin-Ichthyosaur State Park near Gabbs; open camping on BLM land
Finding the site: From Site 74, located off US 95 outside Luning, go up the hill and around to the left for 0.1 mile to a flat parking area on the left.

Rockhounding

The hill behind the parking area is filled with still more specimens of malachite and azurite. Keep stooping and picking until you find the best.

Coaldale: White Quartz, Selenite

Land type: Mountains, mine tailings
Elevation: 5,337 feet
GPS: N38 06.06' / W117 52.58'
Best season: Spring and fall
Land manager: BLM
Material: White quartz, selenite
Tools: Rock hammer
Vehicle: High clearance
Special attractions: None
Accommodations: Motels and RV parking in Hawthorne and Tonopah; open camping on BLM land

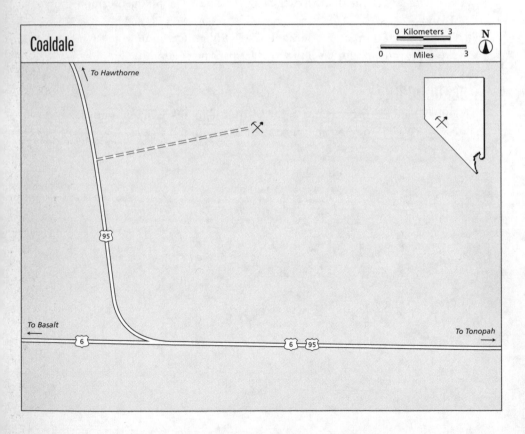

Finding the site: From the junction of US 6 and US 95 at Coaldale Junction, drive north on US 95 for 4.5 miles to a dirt road going right. Follow the dirt road for 2.4 miles to the mine and the tailings piles.

Rockhounding

Hunt all over the tailings for the white quartz and selenite. There is quite a bit of it, and if you are a mineral collector, you will probably find a lot of other goodies here. It is an easy site to get to if—and that's a big *if*—you have a high-clearance vehicle.

Basalt: Petrified Wood, Jasper

Land type: Desert wash
Elevation: 6,400 feet
GPS: N38 00.54' / W118 14.16'
Best season: Spring and fall
Land manager: BLM
Material: Petrified wood, jasper
Tools: Rock hammer
Vehicle: Any
Special attractions: None
Accommodations: Motels and private RV parking in Tonopah; open camping on BLM land
Finding the site: The shortest way to reach this site is to drive west of Tonopah on US 6 for about 56 miles. At this point NV 264 goes south. Keep west on US 6 for another 1.4 miles. Here you will see an old blacktop road forking to the left. Turn onto the old highway and proceed for 0.7 mile. Park off the road and hunt in the wash to the right.

NOTE: When I was researching for the second edition, the entrance to the old blacktop was very rough and rutted. It is possible with a high-clearance vehicle, but be careful not to slide into the ruts. Of course, when you get to the site, it may be better or worse.

Rockhounding

This is another site that I thought about leaving out of this second edition. The material is very scarce, but what I did find was spectacular. The wood casts seem to come from the strange, honeycombed eastern wall of the wash. It will take some serious climbing and digging to find them, but you will be very happy if you are successful. I was lucky. I found a beautiful large piece of

Petrified wood from Basalt. The wood is black with yellow patterns.

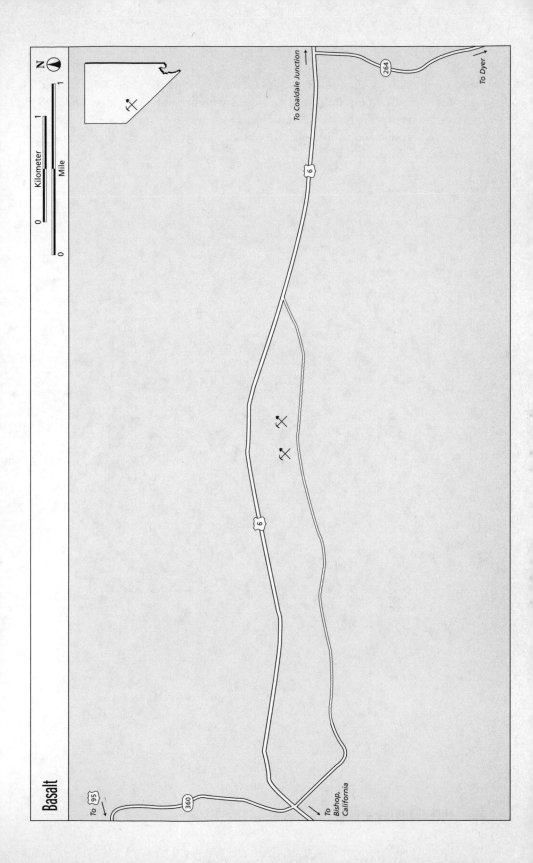

Basalt

N

Kilometer
0   1

Mile
0   1

To 95

360

To Bishop,
California

To

6

6

To Coaldale Junction

264

To Dyer

wood on the floor of the wash and climbed up, following the chips, to get the rest. Not only was it beautiful, but it fluoresces with bright green streaks under shortwave ultraviolet light. I wish you luck. Don't use my name in vain if you go away empty-handed. Remember, it was an easy site to get to (except for that entrance off US 6).

The Sump (Upper): Wood Casts

Land type: Hills
Elevation: 5,500 feet
GPS: N37 56.17' / W118 04.39'
Best season: Spring and fall
Land manager: BLM
Material: Petrified wood casts
Tools: Rock hammer
Vehicle: High clearance
Special attractions: None
Accommodations: Motels and private RV parking in Tonopah; open camping on BLM land
Finding the site: From the intersection of US 95 and US 6 at Coaldale Junction, drive west on US 6 for 6.2 miles to the junction of US 6 and NV 773. Go south on NV 773. At 0.2 mile, you will come to a fork. Keep right. At 7.8 miles (from US 6), you will come to a track going left. Follow this track for about 0.5 mile to the top of the hill. Park and walk to the right to look down into the sump.

Rockhounding

You can wander all over the tops of the hills here and find little white limb and twig casts. Many have very nice definition but they are brittle, so be careful to handle them accordingly. The casts were even scarcer when the second edition was researched, but at least you only had to drive 0.5 mile off the pavement, and the view down into the sump is worth the trip.

The Sump (Upper), The Sump (Lower), Fish Lake Valley

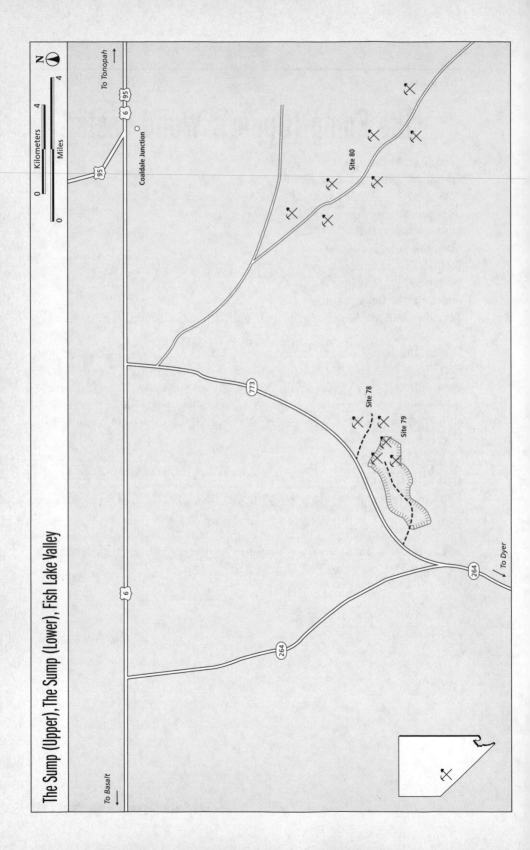

To Basalt

6

264

264

To Dyer

773

Site 78

Site 79

Site 80

95

6 95

95

Coaldale Junction

To Tonopah

N

Kilometers 0   4
Miles   0   4

The Sump (Lower): Petrified Wood

See map on page 182.
Land type: Deep wash
Elevation: 5,300 feet
GPS: N37 55.14' / W118 06.33' (taken at the turnoff from NV 773)
Best season: Spring and fall
Land manager: BLM
Material: Petrified wood
Tools: Rock hammer
Vehicle: High clearance
Special attractions: None
Accommodations: Motels and private RV parking in Tonopah; open camping on BLM land
Finding the site: From the turnoff to Site 78, continue south on NV 773 for 2 miles. You will be about 0.4 mile from the junction of NV 773 and NV 264.

Formations like this abound in the lower sump.

Turn left on the dirt track and go 0.4 mile to the wide wash. Drive down into the wash (it may be a steep drop), turn left up the wash, and drive 1.5 miles to the end.

The wash is sandy in spots, and the driving conditions are dependent on the weather. I drove all the way in with no problems and did not even come close to needing four-wheel drive. In fact, on the day I did research at the site, a Corvette

The lower sump at Site 79 is covered with petrified wood.

could have made the trip. Don't count on those conditions, though, and watch out for the sand. If you have to call AAA from your cell phone out here, you may hear some colorful words from the dispatcher. (That's assuming your cell phone will get a signal.)

Rockhounding

This is one of the most fascinating spots in Nevada. At the head of the wash are the remains of huge stumps. Chips of wood are eroding out and cascading down the mounds. Add the multicolored walls of the wash and the strange eroded shapes standing among the stumps, and you have a place that you just have to add to your itinerary. This sight would be well worth hiking the whole 1.5 miles if you couldn't drive in.

A lot of other material has been reported here. Agate, jasper, and fossils are among them. If you can spare the time, hunt the walls and floor of the wash for the whole length.

Fish Lake Valley: Apache Tears

See map on page 182.
Land type: Desert, hills
Elevation: 5,000 feet
GPS: N37 55.95' / W117 58.91'
Best season: Spring and fall
Land manager: BLM
Material: Apache tears
Tools: None
Vehicle: Any
Special attractions: None
Accommodations: Motels and private RV parking in Tonopah; open camping on
BLM land
Finding the site: From the intersection of US 95 and US 6 at Coaldale Junction,
drive west on US 6 for 6.2 miles to the junction of US 6 and NV 773. Go south
on NV 773 for 0.2 mile to a fork. Take the left fork for 4.7 miles to another
fork. Keep right. From this point, for about 5 miles, you can find Apache tears
on both sides of the road.

Rockhounding

If you don't see any Apache tears where you start, just move on 0.5 mile or so
and try again. It helps to keep the sun at your back. The little black gems will
really twinkle in the sunlight. At first you may have trouble seeing them, but once
you find one, you will see them everywhere.

This nice chunk of pumice is from the Fish Lake Valley site.

Blair Junction: Petrified Wood

Land type: Flat desert
Elevation: 4,900 feet
GPS: N38 01.14' / W117 46.53'
Best season: Spring through fall
Land manager: BLM

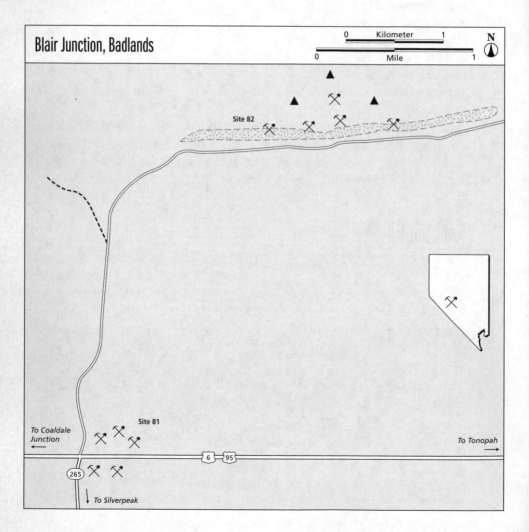

Blair Junction, Badlands

Material: Petrified wood
Tools: None
Vehicle: Any
Special attractions: None
Accommodations: Motels and private RV parking in Tonopah; open camping on BLM land
Finding the site: From Tonopah, drive west on US 6/95 for 34 miles to the junction of US 6/95 and NV 265. Turn onto the dirt road on the north side of the route and park on the flat.

Rockhounding

Small but very nice samples of silicified wood can be found for quite a distance on both sides of the dirt road. Even though this is right next to a well-traveled highway, and there is an unofficial rest stop on the south side, the wood is reasonably abundant. You will have to do a little more walking and stooping than I did for the first edition, but there is still some nice material here. This is a good leg stretcher if you have been driving a long time, and also a good place for the kids to let off a little steam.

Badlands: Agate, Wood, Chalcedony

See map on page 186.

Land type: Deep desert washes
Elevation: 5,300 feet
GPS: N38 03.58' / W117 46.93'
Best season: Spring and fall
Land manager: BLM
Material: Agate, petrified wood, chalcedony, calcite
Tools: Rock hammer
Vehicle: High clearance
Special attractions: None
Accommodations: Motels and private RV parking in Tonopah; open camping on BLM land
Finding the site: From Site 81, continue on the road heading north from US 6/95 near the junction with NV 265. Travel for 1.5 miles to a fork. Keep right and proceed another 1.6 miles. Park in the wide flat next to the big wash.

Rockhounding

This is a very large collecting area. It covers the washes, the sides of the wash, and the low rolling hills. If you are lucky, you will see where others have high-graded their finds at the parking area. This will give you some idea of just what to look for. The hills and the eroded colorful formations make this a good spot to break out the camera. Maybe you can get a shot of yourself with a giant chunk of (fill in the blank with your favorite rock), with the badlands in the background.

Petrified wood specimen from Badlands, Site 82.

Crow Springs A: Apache Tears, Obsidian, Petrified Wood

Land type: Sage-covered desert
Elevation: 4,900 feet
GPS: N38 13.93'/ W117 35.01'

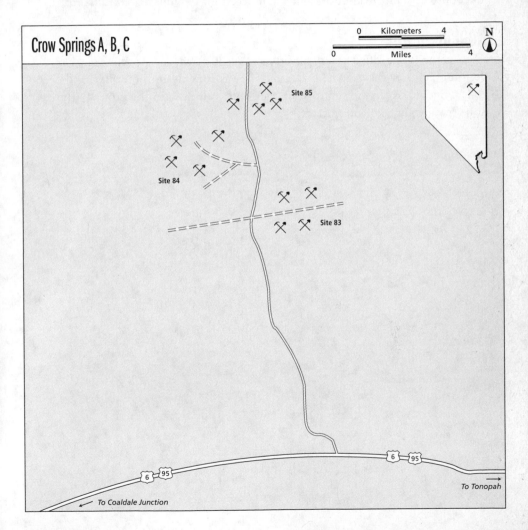

Best season: Spring and fall
Land manager: BLM
Material: Obsidian, petrified wood, Apache tears
Tools: Rock hammer
Vehicle: Any
Special attractions: None
Accommodations: Motels and private RV parking in Tonopah; open camping on BLM land
Finding the site: From Miller's rest area on US 6/95 west of Tonopah, go 7.1 miles west to a road going right. Follow this road for 7 miles to a four-way junction with a dirt road. Turn right and proceed for 0.8 mile. Park off the road.

Rockhounding

Small pieces of petrified wood, small pieces of obsidian, and Apache tears can be found all over this area. The parking place is roughly in the center of the collecting area. Keep the sun to your back and your nose to the ground. (But don't let anyone take your picture.)

Crow Springs B: Apache Tears, Perlite

See map on page 189.

Land type: Hills, old mine
Elevation: 5,400 feet
GPS: N38 14.03' / W117 36.35'
Best season: Spring and fall
Land manager: BLM
Material: Apache tears, perlite
Tools: Rock hammer
Vehicle: Any
Special attractions: None
Accommodations: Motels and private RV parking in Tonopah; open camping on BLM land
Finding the site: From the four-way junction/turnoff to Crow Springs A, continue on the main road for another 1.2 miles. At this point, a road goes left to some obvious old mine workings, which are about 100 yards or so away. Drive up the road and park near the tailings piles.

Rockhounding

I found this site while looking for wood and obsidian in the general area of Crow Springs. I wasn't prepared for what I found, though. As I started toward the mine, I noticed that the road was black, but that didn't ring a bell until I looked at the berm alongside the road. The entire berm was a pile of small obsidian "beads." When I got to the mine, I realized that the tailings piles consisted of both the beads and Apache tears. There were literally mountains of them. A little investigation revealed that it was an old perlite mine. The perlite was the matrix for the tears. Evidently the miners wanted perlite, and they had no use for little hunks of obsidian.

As I walked around the pits, I could see that the walls were light gray perlite sparkling with bits of obsidian. What a sight. Revisited during my research for the second edition, the mine was still abandoned and didn't look much different than it did when I first found it years ago.

Crow Springs C: Petrified Wood, Apache Tears

See map on page 189.
Land type: Sage–covered desert
Elevation: 5,300 feet
GPS: N38 15.31' / W117 37.10'
Best season: Spring and fall
Land manager: BLM
Material: Petrified wood, obsidian
Tools: Rock hammer
Vehicle: Any
Special attractions: None
Accommodations: Motels and private RV parking in Tonopah; open camping on BLM land

Cora walks on a veritable mountain of Apache tears.

Finding the site: From the turn to the mine at Crow Springs B, continue down the main road for another 1.5 miles. Park as far off the road as you can.

Rockhounding

This is another site for wood and obsidian. There is more wood here, and the pieces are a little bigger than the ones at Crow Springs A. Both the wood and obsidian are scattered, so plan on doing a little walking to find the best stuff.

Gabbs Pole Line Road: Plant Fossils

Land type: Small hills
Elevation: 5,000 feet
GPS: N38 09.74' / W117 19.89'
Best season: Spring and fall
Land manager: BLM

Gabbs Pole Line Road

0 Kilometers 2

0 Miles 2

N

Gabbs Pole Line Road

To Coaldale Junction

To Tonopah

6 95

Material: Plant fossils
Tools: Rock hammer, splitting tools
Vehicle: Any
Special attractions: None
Accommodations: Parking for RVs and motels in Tonopah; open camping on BLM land
Finding the site: From the Nye/Esmeralda County line sign on US 6/95 at the west end of Tonopah, go 3.4 miles west to the well-marked Gabbs Pole Line Road. Take this road northwest for 5.1 miles. At this point some tracks go right toward some low hills. There are a couple of tracks, and it doesn't matter which set you take. Drive about 0.2 mile to the hills, pull off the road, and park.

Plant fossil material from the Gabbs Pole Line Road site.

Rockhounding

These are mostly just small broken pieces and imprints of organic material. They are not the most wonderful in the world, but if you are a fossil collector, you might just want some for your collection. It is an easy site to get to on a paved road, and it is near town. You might just get lucky and find a full leaf—or not.

Tonopah A: Agate

Land type: Hills
Elevation: 5,650 feet
GPS: N38 04.45' / W117 10.13'
Best season: Spring and fall
Land manager: BLM
Material: Agate, petrified wood
Tools: Rock hammer
Vehicle: High clearance
Special attractions: None
Accommodations: Motels and private RV parking in Tonopah; open camping on BLM land
Finding the site: From the junction of US 6 and US 95 at the east end of Tonopah, drive east on US 6 for 3 miles to a track going left. Turn onto the track, go through the gate (be sure to leave it as you found it), and continue on for 0.3 mile to the top of the hill. Pull off the track and park.

Rockhounding

Hunt all over the little hills and on the flats. There is a lot of agate here, and you will not have to walk far to find it. The pieces are somewhat small, but there are still some that will cut into 30 x 40 mm cabochons.

Fine petrified wood specimens from Tonopah A, Site 87.

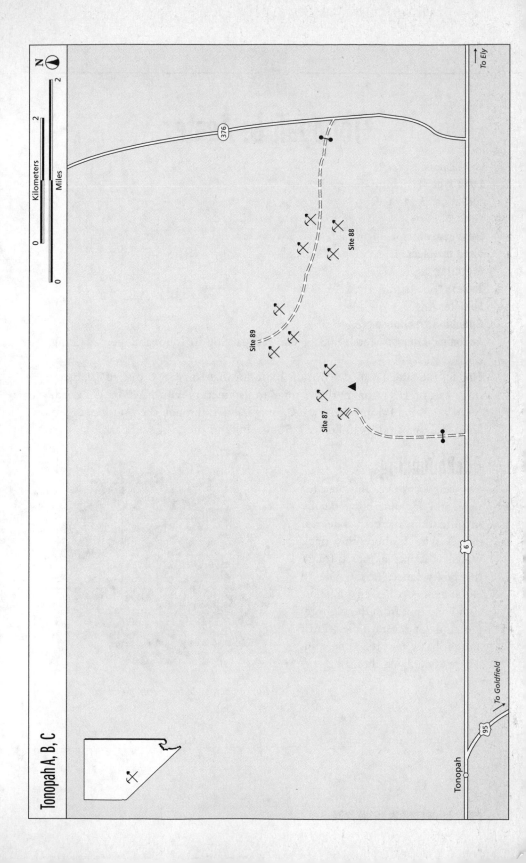

Tonopah A, B, C

Site 87
Site 88
Site 89

376

To Ely

To Goldfield

Tonopah

95

6

N

Kilometers
0   2

Miles
0   2

Tonopah B: Agate

See map on page 197.

Land type: Flat, high desert
Elevation: 5,545 feet
GPS: N38 05.44' / W117 07.78'
Best season: Spring and fall
Land manager: BLM
Material: Agate
Tools: Rock hammer
Vehicle: Any
Special attractions: None
Accommodations: Motels and private RV parking in Tonopah; open camping on BLM land
Finding the site: From the turnoff to Tonopah A on US 6 east of Tonopah, drive east on US 6 for another 3 miles to its junction with NV 376. Go north on NV 376 for 1.3 miles to a track going left. Go through the gate (be sure to leave it as you find it) and drive 0.5 mile. Pull off the track and park.

Rockhounding

You can roam over this area for miles and find nice, but generally small, cutting material. The real reason why I chose this track was that it had a gate through the pesky fence. If you like to climb fences, you can pick just about any spot from the highway junction for several miles north and probably find the same stuff. There—you have choices!

Multicolored agate from Tonopah B.

Tonopah C: Agate

See map on page 197.
Land type: Flat desert
Elevation: 5,750 feet
GPS: N38 05.45' / W117 08.04'
Best season: Spring and fall
Land manager: BLM
Material: Agate, petrified wood
Tools: Rock hammer
Vehicle: High clearance
Special attractions: None
Accommodations: Motels and private RV parking in Tonopah; open camping on BLM land
Finding the site: From Tonopah B, off NV 376, continue up the track for another 0.2 mile and park.

Rockhounding

This has much the same material as Tonopah B, but it is a little more plentiful. This whole area is very large, and it will take some walking and stooping to get the best. The material is not as abundant as it was when I did the first edition, but it is still here.

Lida Junction A: Chalcedony

Land type: Flat desert
Elevation: 4,723 feet
GPS: N37 31.91' / W117 10.05'
Best season: Spring and fall
Land manager: BLM
Material: Chalcedony
Tools: Rock hammer
Vehicle: Any
Special attractions: None
Accommodations: Motels and private RV parking in Tonopah and Beatty; open camping on BLM land
Finding the site: From the junction of NV 266 and US 95 between Tonopah and Beatty, drive north on US 95 for 0.2 mile to a dirt road going right. Fol-

A tribute to the "bad hair day" chalcedony typically found at the Lida Junction sites.

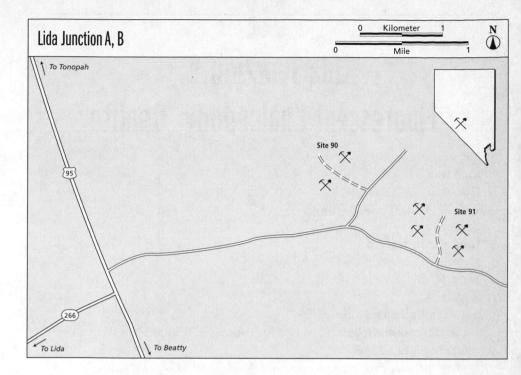

0   Kilometer   1

0   Mile   1

N

To Tonopah

Site 90

95

Site 91

266

To Lida

To Beatty

low this road for 1.8 miles to a fork. Take the left fork for 0.2 mile to a track going left. Turn onto the track and park.

Rockhounding

This is the ugly chalcedony center of the universe. It is primarily a bubbly chalcedony, but is in some grotesque twisted shapes. It is obvious to me that Mother Nature was having a very bad hair day when she created this stuff. If you enjoy one of her jokes, you can probably make a nice conversation piece out of some of these warty specimens. I mounted a particularly warty piece on a mahogany base just for fun. I may send it to my favorite politician.

By the way, just to show that ugly is as ugly does, some of this stuff does fluoresce a deep green under shortwave ultraviolet light.

Lida Junction B:
Fluorescent Chalcedony, Opalite

See map on page 201.
Land type: Flat desert
Elevation: 4,700 feet
GPS: N37 32.00' / W117 09.83'
Best season: Spring and fall
Land manager: BLM
Material: Fluorescent chalcedony, opalite
Tools: Rock hammer
Vehicle: Any
Special attractions: None
Accommodations: Motels and private RV parking in Tonopah and Beatty; open camping on BLM land
Finding the site: From the junction of NV 266 and US 95 between Tonopah and Beatty, drive north on US 95 for 0.2 mile to a dirt road going right. Take this road for 1.8 miles to a fork. Take the right fork for 0.4 mile to a dirt track going left. Pull onto the track and park.

Rockhounding

There are small pieces of bubbly chalcedony and equally small pieces of whitish opalite scattered over a wide area. As beauty goes, they are far from remarkable, but many of them do fluoresce a very pretty green under shortwave ultraviolet light.

Lida Junction C: Fluorescent Chalcedony

Land type: Flat desert
Elevation: 4,800 feet
GPS: N37 26.431' / W117 16.260'
Best season: Spring through fall
Land manager: BLM
Material: Fluorescent chalcedony
Tools: Rock hammer
Vehicle: Any
Special attractions: Old mining town of Gold Point nearby
Accommodations: Motels and private RV parking in Tonopah and Beatty; open camping on BLM land
Finding the site: From the intersection of US 95 and NV 266 between Tonopah and Beatty, drive west on NV 266 for 6.3 miles. At this point a dirt track goes left toward some low hills. There is a rather sharp dip at the entrance to the track. If your vehicle can make the dip, you can drive quite a way toward the hills in any vehicle. The collecting begins at only 0.1 mile from NV 266, so if you can't make the dip, just park along the road and hike in.

NOTE: This is a site that I completely overlooked on two trips. Don't ask how I did that. The simplest thing would have been just to forget it, but Cora and I had a lot of fun at this site when we did the first edition, and I'd like you to have some too. Consequently, I have put it in the second edition with GPS coordinates that I pulled from a topo map. I'm pretty sure that they are within yards of the dirt track, but the 6.3-mile marker from the highway junction will put you there anyway. It's a short trip from US 95 down a nice paved road, and the area is vast. The hunting starts right by the road and stretches to the nearby mountain. Give it a try and let me know how you make out.

Fluorescent chalcedony from Lida Junction C (Site 92).

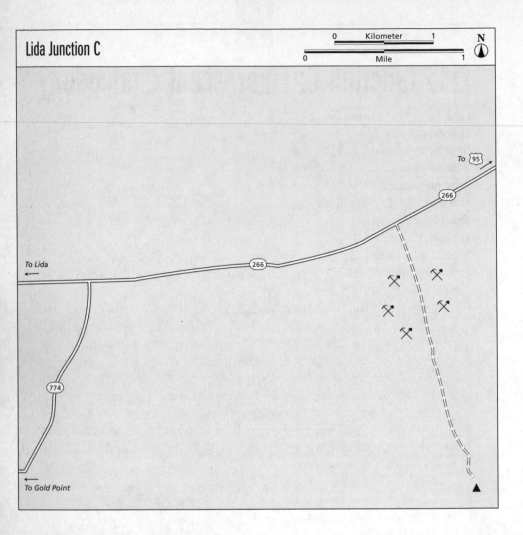

0   Kilometer   1

0   Mile   1

N

To 95

266

To Lida
←

266

774

To Gold Point
←

▲

Rockhounding

Small, bubbly pieces of clear chalcedony are scattered all over this area. Many are very pretty in daylight, and some look like broken geode halves. A bonus is that most of them fluoresce a bright green under shortwave ultraviolet light. If you are in a hiking mood, walk toward the low hills to the south. Agate and petrified wood have been reported in this area, and you just might get lucky.

Stonewall Pass A: Petrified Wood, Chalcedony

Land type: Mountains
Elevation: 5,171 feet
GPS: N37 23.28' / W117 13.77'
Best season: Spring and fall
Land manager: BLM
Material: Petrified wood, chalcedony
Tools: Rock hammer
Vehicle: High clearance
Special attractions: None
Accommodations: Motels and private RV parking in Tonopah and Beatty; open camping on BLM land

Petrified wood and chalcedony can be found on the flats, in the washes, and on the flanks of the hills at Stonewall Pass A.

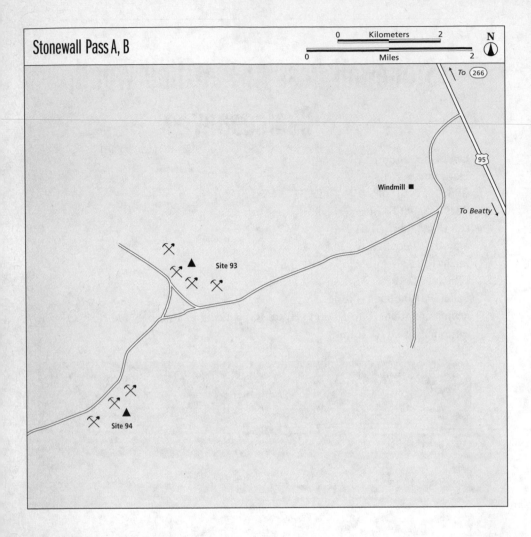

Kilometers

Miles

N

To 266

95

Windmill ■

To Beatty

Site 93

Site 94

Finding the site: From the junction of US 95 and NV 266 between Tonopah and Beatty, drive south on US 95 for 3.4 miles to a road going right. Follow this road for 0.7 mile to a fork. To the right, you will see an old windmill. Take the right fork and continue on for another 5 miles. Here a dirt road goes right. Take this road for 0.1 mile and park on the flat to the left of the gray ash hills.

Rockhounding

Hunt all over the area around the ash hills. I had the best luck on the south side of the hills and in a little wash. You will see where others have dug, and you can use their tailings to get an idea of what you are looking for. There are some nice pieces of chalcedony and some equally good pieces of petrified wood. A definite plus is finding nice pieces of wood, which fluoresce in a green fortification pattern.

Petrified wood from Stonewall Pass A.

This is an old area, so you will have to do some serious stooping and throwing to get good material. Your work may pay off, though. Some beautiful wood has been taken out of here, and it is unlikely that it is all gone.

Stonewall Pass B: Wood Casts, Agate, Chalcedony, Jasper

See map on page 206.
Land type: Mountains
Elevation: 5,379 feet
GPS: N37 22.55' / W117 13.84'
Best season: Spring and fall
Land manager: BLM
Material: Wood casts, agate, jasper, chalcedony
Tools: Rock hammer
Vehicle: High clearance
Special attractions: None
Accommodations: Motels and private RV parking in Tonopah and Beatty; open camping on BLM land
Finding the site: From the turnoff to Site 93, 5 miles down the road from the first fork near the windmill, continue up left on the road for another 0.9 mile. Pull off to the left and park on the flat next to the low hills.

Rockhounding

There is a lot of material around and on the low hills. Petrified wood occurs as a cast of soft, whitish silica. The stuff is very brittle, so be very careful with it. When it weathers out, it doesn't take long for it to dissolve into mush. A little searching and careful digging will get you some very pretty specimens, though. There is also agate, jasper, and clear chalcedony here. Do a little walking and a lot of stooping and you will come away happy. You will be even happier if you find some of the green fluorescing material.

Petrified wood specimens from Stonewall Pass B.

Scotty's Junction A: Apache Tears

Land type: Flat desert
Elevation: 4,200 feet
GPS: N37 12.50' / W116 57.64'
Best season: Spring through fall
Land manager: BLM

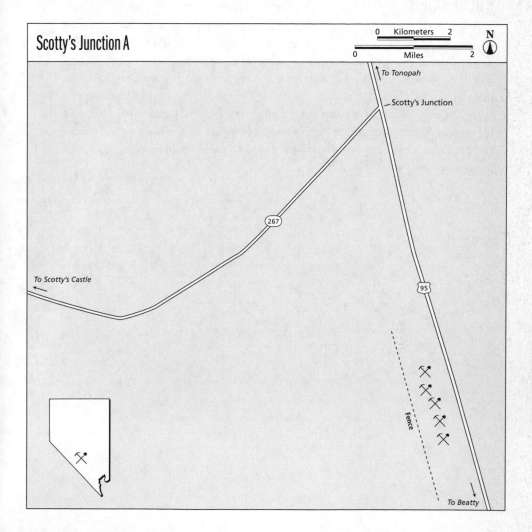

Scotty's Junction A

0   Kilometers   2
0   Miles   2
N

To Tonopah

Scotty's Junction

267

To Scotty's Castle

95

Fence

To Beatty

Material: Apache tears
Tools: None
Vehicle: Any
Special attractions: Scotty's Castle
Accommodations: Motels and private RV parking in Tonopah and Beatty; open camping on BLM land
Finding the site: From the junction of US 95 and NV 267 (Scotty's Junction), about 36 miles north of Beatty, drive south on US 95 for about 8 or 9 miles. Find a place to pull off the highway and park.

Rockhounding

This is a place where you can stretch your legs and pick up some Apache tears at the same time. The highway is fenced along here, and there are no gates, so your collecting will have to be done between the pavement and the fence. There is plenty of room and there are plenty of tears, but you will have to keep an eye on the kids since the traffic on US 95 can go pretty fast along this lonely stretch. If you have some time and want a little safer place to hunt, give the sites at Scotty's Junction B and D a try. They are in the same field of tears (Is that like a field of dreams?), but are inside the fence where there is a lot of room to roam.

Scotty's Junction B: Apache Tears

Land type: Flat desert
Elevation: 4,029 feet
GPS: N37 17.35' / W117 02.68'
Best season: Spring and fall
Land manager: BLM
Material: Apache tears
Tools: None
Vehicle: Any
Special attractions: Scotty's Castle
Accommodations: Motels and RV parking in Beatty; open camping on BLM land
Finding the site: From the junction of US 95 and NV 267 (Scotty's Junction), about 36 miles north of Beatty, drive west on NV 267 for about 100 yards. Here a dirt road goes left. Follow this road for about 0.2 mile to a fork. Take the left fork for 0.6 mile. Park and hunt all over the area.

Rockhounding

There are bazillions of Apache tears here, but they occur in patches, so if you don't see any right away, move a little and try again. As with all Apache tear hunting, keep the sun at your back and look for the little twinkles. Once you get the knack, you will see them everywhere.

Scotty's Junction B, C, D

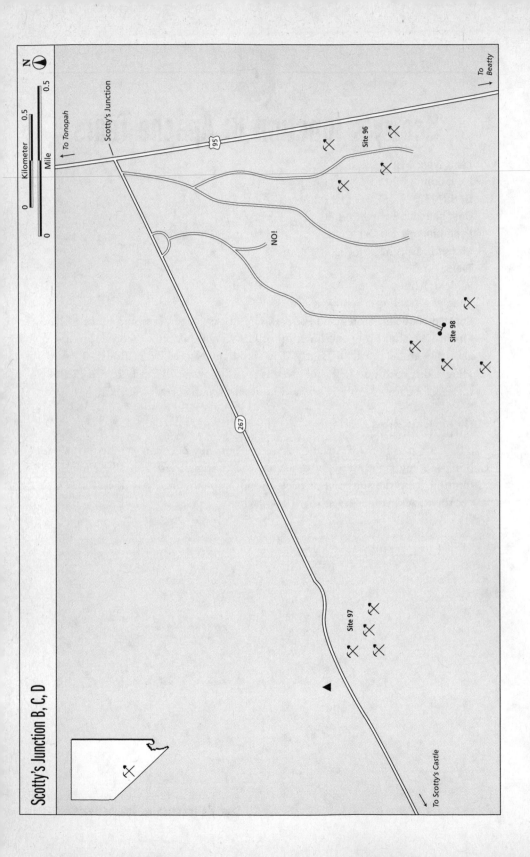

Scotty's Junction C: Chalcedony, Apache Tears, Pumice

See map on page 212.
Land type: Flat desert
Elevation: 4,036 feet
GPS: N37 16.71' / W117 05.03'
Best season: Spring through fall
Land manager: BLM
Material: Chalcedony, Apache tears, pumice
Tools: None
Vehicle: Any
Special attractions: Scotty's Castle
Accommodations: Motels and private RV parking in Beatty; open camping on BLM land
Finding the site: From the junction of US 95 and NV 267 (Scotty's Junction), about 36 miles north of Beatty, drive west on NV 267 for 2.2 miles. At this point, there is a big gravel pile on the right-hand side of the road. Park near it or on it and hunt on both sides of the road.

This pumice from Scotty's Junction C looks so much like wood.

Rockhounding

There are chalcedony and Apache tears here, but they are not plentiful. The real prize is the pumice. Did I say pumice? Why would anyone want to collect pumice? Well, I confess that when I first found these little jewels, I thought they were wood casts, but the experts told me they were pumice. They are light brown or tan in color and are fairly soft, but the detail is exceptional. Most of the pieces are only an inch or two long and about as wide. It is rather easy to find pieces that show what appear to be tiny knots and great grain patterns. Some of the material is badly weathered, but don't despair. There is plenty of the good stuff. I found material on both sides of the road, but it seems to be much more plentiful on the south side. Here is a golden opportunity to be the first kids on your block to start a pumice collection.

Scotty's Junction D: Apache Tears

See map on page 212.
Land type: Flat desert
Elevation: 4,019 feet
GPS: N37 17.28' / W117 02.91'
Best season: Spring through fall
Land manager: BLM
Material: Apache tears
Tools: None
Vehicle: Any
Special attractions: Scotty's Castle
Accommodations: Motels and private RV parking in Beatty; open camping on BLM land
Finding the site: From the junction of US 95 and NV 267 (Scotty's Junction), about 36 miles north of Beatty, drive west on NV 267 for 0.2 mile. Follow the track to the left for 0.8 mile to a dead end. Park and hunt all over the flats.

Rockhounding

Apache tears are scattered all over a large area.

Beatty: Fluorescent Chalcedony

Land type: Hills
Elevation: 3,450 feet
GPS: N36 57.69' / W116 42.76'
Best season: Spring through fall
Land manager: BLM

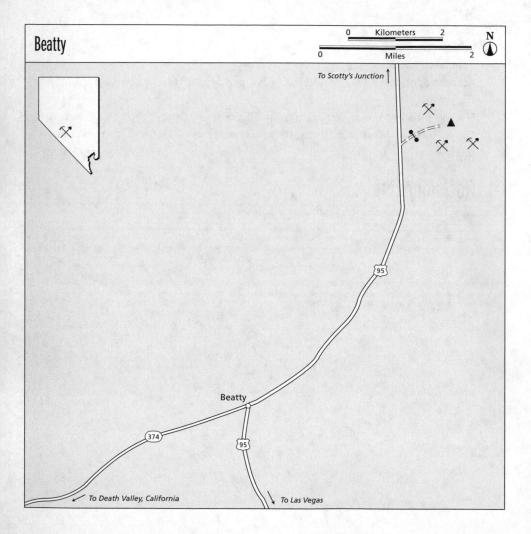

Beatty

Material: Fluorescent chalcedony
Tools: Rock hammer
Vehicle: Any
Special attractions: Old Bullfrog mining district
Accommodations: Motels and private RV parking in Beatty
Finding the site: From the junction of US 95 and NV 374 in Beatty, drive north on US 95 for 4.5 miles. At this point, you will see a dirt road with a closed gate on the right. Go through the gate (be sure to close it behind you) and proceed straight ahead toward the little rocky ridge for 0.1 mile. Park in any convenient spot and hunt on the slopes of the ridge.

Rockhounding

There are still plenty of nice little pieces of bubbly clear chalcedony all over the slopes. Many fluoresce a nice green under shortwave ultraviolet light.

Carrara A: Blue-Gray Quartz

Land type: Desert hills
Elevation: 3,800 feet
GPS: N36 49.53' / W116 42.54'
Best season: Spring and fall
Land manager: BLM
Material: Blue-gray quartz
Tools: Rock hammer
Vehicle: High clearance
Special attractions: None
Accommodations: Motels and private RV parking in Beatty; open camping on BLM land
Finding the site: From the junction of US 95 and NV 374 in Beatty, drive south on US 95 for 7.1 miles to a road going left. Follow this dirt road past

Deserted buildings mark the start of the road to Carrara A.

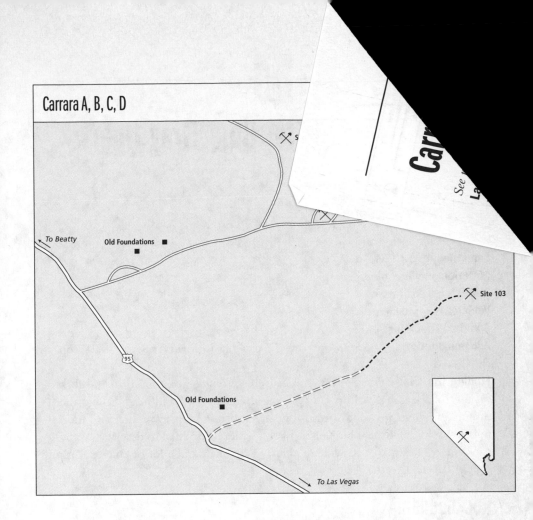

Carrara A, B, C, D

To Beatty

Old Foundations ■

Site 103

95

Old Foundations ■

To Las Vegas

some old foundations for 1.6 miles. At this point you will come to a fork. Take the left fork toward the obvious workings on the mountain ahead. Drive as close to the workings as you can and park.

Rockhounding

Walk up the road to the mine and keep an eye out all along the road for some good-size pieces of blue-gray quartz. There are tons of it here, and some of it will make nice lapidary material. There are other mineral specimens around, so be on the lookout for all kinds of things. This was a fairly large operation, and you can walk along the edge of the hill where the old mine car tracks used to run. The walls along the old track are filled with seams of quartz.

ara B: Phyllite, Blue-Gray Quartz

ap on page 219.

d type: Desert hills

Elevation: 3,800 feet

GPS: N36 49.99' / W116 41.97'

Best season: Spring and fall

Land manager: BLM

Material: Phyllite, blue-gray quartz

Tools: Rock hammer

Vehicle: High clearance

Special attractions: None

Accommodations: Motels and private RV parking in Beatty; open camping on BLM land

Finding the site: From the mine at Site 100, retrace your route to the fork on the road leading back to US 95. Take the right fork and head around the mountain. There are a lot of roads out here, so just keep to the left and head for the backside of the mountain. It is a lot easier to do than to describe. At the backside of the mine, you will see a fenced-off shaft and a lot of tailings. Park on the flat next to the shaft.

Rockhounding

Search throughout the area for phyllite and more of the blue-gray quartz. If you are lucky, you may even find some pieces of white marble.

Carrara C: White Quartz, Marble, Blue-Gray Quartz

See map on page 219.
Land type: Desert, mountains
Elevation: 3,637 feet
GPS: N36 49.84' / W116 41.98'
Best season: Spring through fall
Land manager: BLM
Material: White quartz, marble, blue-gray quartz
Tools: Rock hammer
Vehicle: High clearance
Special attractions: None
Accommodations: Motels and private RV parking in Beatty; open camping on BLM land
Finding the site: From the mine at Site 100, retrace your route to the fork in the road leading to the sites from US 95. Take the right fork and drive 0.4 mile to a track going left. Follow the track for 0.1 mile, turn right, and park. Roam around, stoop, and toss. There is a lot to be gathered out here.

Rockhounding

This is a fertile area for the rockhound. The farther you roam and the more time you spend, the more you will take home.

Carrara D: Marble

See map on page 219.

Land type: Desert, mountains
Elevation: 3,100 feet (at the highway)
GPS: N36 47.92' / W116 42.73' (at the US 95 turnoff)
Best season: Spring through fall
Land manager: BLM
Material: White marble
Tools: Rock hammer, heavy hammers, chisels
Vehicle: Four-wheel drive
Special attractions: None
Accommodations: Motels and private RV parking in Beatty; open camping on BLM land
Finding the site: From US 95 at the turnoff to the other Carrara sites (south of Beatty), continue south on US 95 for 1.3 miles. Here a road goes left past some old foundations. There isn't much left of the foundations, and they are a little hard to see from the highway, so keep your eyes peeled. As you pull off the highway and look eastward toward the mountains, you will see the road running straight as a string across the desert. It is only about 2.5 miles to the quarry, and the road starts out as a reasonably good graded track. Trust me, it is not.

The first mile or so will lull you into complacency. At about 1 mile you will come to a washout. It is not terrible, and the road beyond looks good. At this point, I gambled and crossed the washout. From that point on, the washouts became the norm and the decent road disappeared. The track is in a depression, and it is extremely difficult and sometimes impossible to turn around for about 1 mile beyond the first washout. That mile is just about the most miserable one I have driven. It got so bad that I got within 0.5 mile of the quarry and gave up. That is almost unheard of for me, but this time I had had it. I might have continued for some really nice agate. I might have kept on for turquoise or precious opal, but for white marble, no way. If you try it, I understand that you can get to within 0.5 or 0.25 mile of the main workings.

The torturous road to the marble quarry at Carrara. It looks good here, but don't be fooled.

Rockhounding

If you can't live without seeing the quarry and you don't want to drive the torturous path, you can hike the 1.5 miles or so from the end of the easily passable road to the site. If you just want some marble samples to play with, there are tons of them all along the road from the highway on. When I was there, there were still several huge blocks of nice, pure white marble right next to the highway by the old foundations. Get out the sledge and knock off a few pieces.

Valley of Fire A: Wonderstone

Land type: Desert, mountains
Elevation: 2,655 feet
GPS: N36 23.86' / W114 41.70'
Best season: Spring and fall
Land manager: BLM
Material: Wonderstone
Tools: Rock hammer
Vehicle: High clearance

The sign points the way to the Valley of Fire sites.

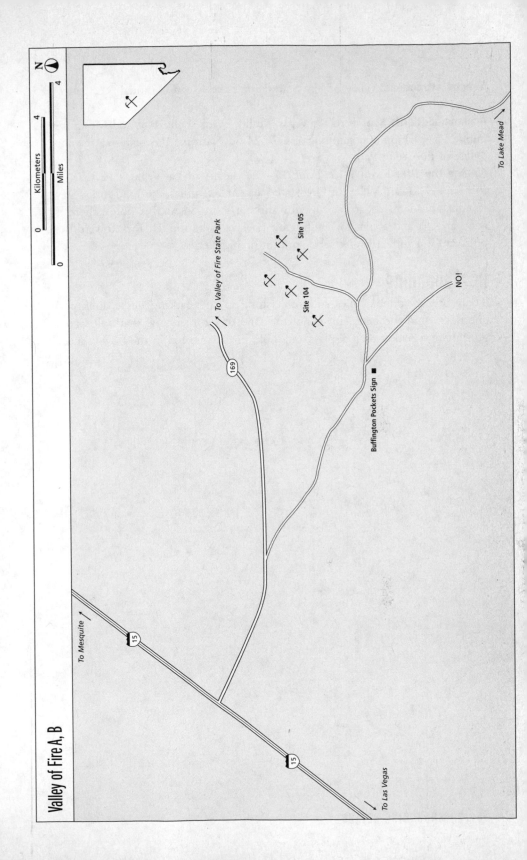

Valley of Fire A, B

N

Kilometers
0   4

Miles
0   4

To Mesquite →

15

To Las Vegas →

15

169 →

To Valley of Fire State Park ↑

Site 104

Site 105

Buffington Pockets Sign ■

NO!

To Lake Mead →

Special attractions: Valley of Fire State Park; Lake Mead National Recreation Area; Hoover Dam

Accommodations: Motels in Las Vegas, Boulder City, Echo Bay, and Mesquite; public RV parking and camping at Lake Mead National Recreation Area and Valley of Fire State Park

Finding the site: From I-15 about 35 miles north of Las Vegas, take exit 75 to NV 169 toward Valley of Fire State Park. At 3.2 miles, the road forks. Stay straight ahead on the right fork for another 4 miles. At this point, there is another fork and a sign for Buffington Pockets. Take the left fork toward the pockets for 1 mile, turn left, and park in the big circle.

Rockhounding

There are several big piles of wonderstone in the parking circle. Pick and choose to find the best. This is not the kind of wonderstone that will take a polish, but it makes nice displays and looks great scattered in the flower beds.

Valley of Fire B: Chalcedony

See map on page 225.
Land type: Desert mountains
Elevation: 2,657 feet
GPS: N36 23.94' / W114 41.42'
Best season: Spring and fall
Land manager: BLM
Material: Chalcedony
Tools: Rock hammer
Vehicle: High clearance
Special attractions: Valley of Fire State Park; Lake Mead National Recreation Area; Hoover Dam
Accommodations: Motels in Las Vegas, Boulder City, Echo Bay, and Mesquite; public RV parking and camping at Lake Mead National Recreation Area and Valley of Fire State Park.
Finding the site: From Site 104, continue on the dirt road for 0.2 mile and park off the road.

Rockhounding

Hunt all over the surrounding area for small chunks of chalcedony. It's not the best, but not the worst either.

Appendix A: Sources for Maps

The maps in this book, when used in conjunction with a standard highway map, will be all that you will need to find the sites. If you wish to go beyond what I have shown, or if you wish to strike out on your own to find that special spot, you will need more detailed maps. Remember, though, that many of the excellent United States Geological Survey topographic maps are twenty years old or older. The old mine roads, and jeep roads—and dirt roads in general—shown on the maps may no longer be there, and many new ones surely will be. This alone is reason enough to get that GPS unit. If you start down the wrong road, you will know it right away and can make corrections. Maps are still important, though, and you should be able to get just about any one you could wish for at one of the following sources.

Pacific West Maps
994 N. Main St.
Orange, CA 92867
(714) 633-0800
www.PacificWestMaps.com
These folks have just about any kind of map you could want. In fact, if they don't have it, you probably don't need it. You can contact them by phone, by mail, or by e-mail, and they will send you what you need.

Nevada Bureau of Mines and Geology
University of Nevada-Reno/178
Reno, NV 89557
(775) 682-8760
Here you can find a wealth of books and pamphlets on mines and geology of Nevada. They also have a nice rockhound's map of the state.

Bureau of Land Management State Office
1340 Financial Blvd./P.O. Box 12000
Reno, NV 89502
(775) 861-6400 (front desk)
e-mail: nvsoweb@blm.gov
BLM district and field offices are listed below. All of the field offices may not have maps, but you can usually get first-hand information on where you want to go from the helpful folks.

Battle Mountain District Office
50 Bastian Rd.
Battle Mountain, NV 89820
(775) 635-4000
e-mail: bmfoweb@blm.gov

Mount Lewis Field Office
50 Bastian Rd.
Battle Mountain, NV 89820
(775) 635-4000

Tonopah Field Office
1553 South Main St./P.O. Box 911
Tonopah, NV 89049
(775) 482-7800

Carson City District Office
5665 Morgan Mill Rd.
Carson City, NV 89701
(775) 885-6000

Sierra Front Field Office
5665 Morgan Mill Rd.
Carson City, NV 89701
(775) 885-6000

Stillwater Field Office
5665 Morgan Mill Rd.
Carson City, NV 89701
(775) 885-6000

Elko District Office
3900 East Idaho St./P.O. Box 831
Elko, NV 89801
(775) 753-0200

Tuscarora Field Office
3900 East Idaho St.
Elko, NV 89801
(775) 753-0200

Wells Field Office
3900 East Idaho St.
Elko, NV 89801
(775) 753-0200

Ely District Office
702 North Industrial Way/HC 33
Box 33500
Ely, NV 89301
(775) 289-1800
e-mail: eyfoweb@blm.gov

Caliente Field Office
US Hwy 93 Bldg #1/P.O. Box 237
Caliente, NV 89008
(775) 726-8100
e-mail: cfoweb@blm.gov

Egan Field Office
702 North Industrial Way/HC 33
Box 33500
Ely, NV 89301
(775) 289-1800
e-mail: eyfoweb@blm.gov

Schell Field Office
702 North Industrial Way/HC 33
Box 33500
Ely, NV 89301
(775) 289-1800
e-mail: eyfoweb@blm.gov

Southern Nevada District Office
4701 North Torrey Pines Dr.
Las Vegas, NV 89130
(702) 515-5000
e-mail: lvfoweb@blm.gov

Las Vegas Field Office
4701 North Torrey Pines Dr.
Las Vegas, NV 89130
(702) 515-5000
e-mail: lvfoweb@blm.gov

Winnemucca District Office
5100 East Winnemucca Blvd.
Winnemucca, NV 89445
(775) 623-5100
e-mail: wfoweb@blm.gov

Pahrump Field Office
4701 North Torrey Pines Dr.
Las Vegas, NV 89130
(702) 515-5000
e-mail: lvfoweb@blm.gov

Black Rock Field Office
5100 East Winnemucca Blvd.
Winnemucca, NV 89445
(775) 623-5100
e-mail: wfoweb@blm.gov

Red Rock/Sloan Field Office
4701 North Torrey Pines Dr.
Las Vegas, NV 89130
(702) 515-5000
e-mail: lvfoweb@blm.gov

Humboldt River Field Office
5100 East Winnemucca Blvd.
Winnemucca, NV 89445
(775) 623-5100
e-mail: wfoweb@blm.gov

The Nevada Department of Transportation has an excellent map book called *The Nevada Map Atlas*. This is my favorite of all of the Nevada maps. It is spiral-bound so that it lies flat, and it contains well-detailed maps that show lots and lots of dirt roads. It can be ordered from the department at:

Nevada Department of Transportation
Map Section, Room 206
1263 South Stewart St.
Carson City, NV 89712
(775) 888-7627

DeLorme publishes a *Nevada Atlas and Gazetteer* that includes topo maps of the entire state. It also shows many dirt roads and is available at most bookstores and rock shops, as well as online at places like Amazon.com.

Appendix B: Glossary

agate: A form of chalcedony containing bands or mossy inclusions. Often very colorful, but sometimes with either one color or very muted colors.

aggregate: A mixture of different kinds of rocks or crystals.

alabaster: A fine-grained variety of gypsum used widely for carving.

amethyst: A gemstone of the quartz family ranging in color from pale lilac to deep purple.

ammonite: A cephalopod fossil curled like a ram's horn.

aquamarine: A form of beryl next in desirability to emerald. Colors range from pale to deep blue or blue green.

azurite: A blue copper carbonate often associated with malachite.

barite: Barium sulfate occurring in blue, green, brown, and red.

beryl: Beryllium aluminum sulfate that is colorless in its pure form. Colored varieties include emerald, green; aquamarine, blue; morganite, pink; and heliodor, brown to golden yellow.

biotite: A member of the mica group usually in black, brown black, or green black.

book: Term for a common occurrence of mica in leaves that resemble the pages of a book.

cabbing: The act of creating a cabochon.

cabochon (cab): A common shape for a gem, usually with an elliptical perimeter and a domed top.

calcite: Calcium carbonate that occurs in clear crystals as well as white, brown, red, yellow, and blue.

cephalopod: Free-swimming marine animal. Ammonites and baculites are typical of cephalopods.

chalcedony: A cryptocrystalline form of quartz in which the crystal structure is not visible to the naked eye. The forms include agate, jasper, carnelian, sard, onyx, chrysoprase, sardonyx, and flint.

chalcedony rose: A chalcedony formation resembling a rose.

concretion: A cemented accumulation of mineral material. Common concretions may contain pyrite, silica, calcite, or gypsum.

coprolite: Fossilized excrement in sedimentary rock.

country rock: The common rock surrounding a vein or other deposit of gemstones or minerals.

crinoid: One of hundreds of round stemlike echinoderms. Usually only parts are found as fossils.

crystal: A solid mineral having a regular geometric shape with flat faces or surfaces.

dendrite: A mineral inclusion in a rock that resembles the branching of a fern.

dike: A wall of igneous rock surrounded by country rock.

epidote: Green crystal sometimes used as a gemstone, but more commonly collected for display.

feldspar: The most abundant minerals in the Earth's crust. The feldspars are classified as orthoclase and plagioclase. Among the most desired varieties are moonstone, sunstone, microcline, and labradorite.

float: Gemstones, minerals, and other such things that have been transported from their place of origin by water, erosion, or gravity.

fluorescence: Colors emitted by many minerals when exposed to ultraviolet light.

fluorite: A common mineral that occurs in colors of white, brown, purple, green, yellow, violet, and blue. Although it is sometimes faceted, it is too soft to stand up to the day-to-day wear given jewelry.

fluorspar: A less pure and more granular form of fluorite.

fortification agate: Agate with acutely banded corners that form a closed figure resembling a fort.

fossils: Remains of plants, insects, or animals preserved in either casts or molds.

gangue: Country rock or other rock of no value surrounding minerals or gemstones.

garnet: A group of differently colored, but chemically similar, minerals. The group includes pyrope, red with brown; almandine, red with violet; spessartite, orange to red brown; grossular, yellow to copper brown; demantoid, emerald green; and uvarovite, emerald green.

gem: A gemstone that has been prepared for use in jewelry.

gemstone: Any precious or semiprecious stone that can be cut and/or polished for jewelry.

geode: A hollow nodule or concretion, usually filled with crystal formations.

gypsum: A hydrous calcium sulfate that occurs in white, colorless, gray, brown, red, and yellow. The colorless variety is called selenite and the dense form is called alabaster.

igneous: One of the three primary classifications of rock, formed by solidification or crystallization of magma.

jasper: Opaque form of chalcedony, often with mossy inclusions or intertwining of various colors.

lapidary: The art of forming and shaping gemstones or one who forms or shapes gemstones.

lepidolite: Pink- to lilac-colored silicate mineral of the mica group.

limonite: A term applied generally to a brownish iron hydroxide. Often occurs as a pseudomorph after iron minerals, such as pyrite.

malachite: A green copper ore that occurs both in crystal and massive forms. The massive forms are often banded, and many contain beautiful bull's-eyes.

massive form: The form of a mineral in which the crystals are either very small or without any discernible definition.

matrix: Material in which a mineral crystal or fossil is embedded.

metamorphic: Preexisting rock changed by the action of pressure, chemical action, or heat. One of the three primary classifications of rock.

mica: A group of sheet silicate minerals whose major members are muscovite, biotite phlogopite, lepidolite, and chlorite.

micromount: A tiny mineral specimen intended for viewing under a microscope.

muscovite: One of the mica group, usually colorless to pale yellow, green, pink, or brown.

onyx: A black-and-white banded chalcedony. The colored varieties sold in gift shops are either dyed onyx or a form of calcite or aragonite.

opal: A silicon oxide closely related to chalcedony, but softer and containing water. Common opal is often dull and not suitable for jewelry, but some have a waxy texture and will cut and polish into nice cabochons. Common opal often replaces wood fibers in fossil wood and makes finely detailed samples. Precious opal is the type associated with fine jewelry and shows beautiful flashes of multicolored fire. It is often mistakenly called fire opal, but true fire opal is red and does not have the flashes of fire.

opalite: An impure form of common opal, also called myrickite.

ozokerite: A hard mineral wax once used widely for everything from waterproofing of matches to making statues for wedding cakes.

pegmatite: Coarse-grained igneous rock, often the host for gemstones and minerals. Usually found as smaller masses in large igneous formations.

pelecypods: Bivalved mollusks with shells that meet evenly at the hinge. The shells are not symmetrical as in the brachiopods. Oysters, clams, and mussels are typical pelecypods.

perlite: A volcanic glass similar to obsidian used for aggregate, insulation, and soil conditioner.

petrification: The process by which silica or other minerals replace the cell structure of organic material.

phyllite: A metamorphic rock similar to shale, but often containing more quartz and feldspars than the shales.

porphry: Rock containing crystals in a fine-grained mass.

pseudomorph: A crystal with the geometric appearance of one mineral, but which has been chemically replaced with another mineral.

pyrite: Iron sulfide or disulfide with a brassy yellow color. Commonly called fools' gold.

quartz (cryptocrystalline): Group that includes amethyst, aventurine, citrine, rose quartz, smoky quartz, and tiger eye.

quartz (macrocrystalline): Group that includes chalcedony, agate, jasper, onyx, chrysoprase, and sard.

rhodochrosite: A manganese carbonate gemstone in colors from rose-red to white with striping. Sometimes forms as stalactites in caves.

rhodonite: A deep red to pink gemstone usually with black manganese oxide inclusions that often appear as spider webbing.

rhyolite: An extrusive igneous rock, primarily composed of quartz and feldspar.

sedimentary: Rock formed by deposition, compaction, and cementation. One of the three primary classifications of rock.

septarian nodule: A spherical concretion with an internal polygonal system of calcite-filled cracks.

silicified: A mineral or organic compound that has been replaced by silica.

tailings: Waste material from mining or milling.

turquoise: A hydrous phosphate of copper and aluminum that occurs in sky-blue, apple-green, and bluish-green colors. Most of the world's turquoise is mined in Nevada.

ultraviolet lamp: A lamp that produces ultraviolet rays that cause colors to be emitted by many minerals.

Index

About the Author

Bill Kappele, author of *The Rockhound's Guide to Colorado* and *Rockhounding Utah,* is a contributing editor at *Rock & Gem* magazine and has been writing field trip and how-to articles for the magazine since 1986. In addition, he has been their Shop Talk columnist since 1995.

Bill has also been rockhound-ing across the western states for more than 40 years. He should have been bitten by the rock bug back in the early 1950s when, after a tour in the Navy during the Korean War, he was assigned to the Naval Auxiliary Air Station at El Centro, California. This was an unlikely place for a sailor, but a paradise for a rockhound. One of the old-timers at the base was a dyed-in-the-wool collector and spent the time when he wasn't picking up the treasures of the desert showing them to the rest of the crew. Too bad Bill didn't have sense enough to follow him to the fire agate beds.

It may well be that the bug really did bite him back then, but it was not until some years later, during summer camping trips with his wife, Cora, and sons, Bill and Richard, that he began feeling the effects. Before long, the garage and back-yard filled with a conglomeration of agate, jasper, "pretty" rocks, and "leaverite" ("Leave 'er right where you found 'er"). In self-defense, he began the second hobby of most rockhounds—lapidary. The pile of rocks started to go down. Some of them became cabochons, some were stored in cabinets and labeled as to type and source, and some became history.

As the piles waxed and waned, the sophistication of the collecting increased, and the camping trips became rockhound trips. There were attempts to hunt in the snow on Hurricane Mesa in Utah, beachcombing trips in sunny Southern California, and backpacking trips in the Mojave Desert. Any place that might have interesting rocks was a place to go. One time, up in Idaho, Bill found some fossil wood where the principal landmark was a dead horse. He wonders if it is still there. (The horse, not the wood.)

When Bill and Cora's younger son, Richard, moved to Henderson, Nevada, a door was opened to yet another state to check out for rocks. In doing the research for the first edition of *Rockhounding Nevada,* Bill and Cora traveled almost 8,000 miles and covered the state from corner to corner and side to side.

Sadly, Cora passed away suddenly in November 2007, so revisiting all the sites was a bittersweet adventure for Bill. He is sure, though, that Cora would have been proud to have seen a second edition in print.